MAA A

Volume III

The Kamitic Shaman Way of Working the
Superconscious Mind to Improve Memory,
Solve Problems Intuitively and Spiritually
Grow Through the Power of the Spirits

Derric "Rau Khu" Moore

Four Sons Publications
Liberal, KS
1solalliance.com

Published by: Four Sons Publications

Contact: 1 SŏL Alliance Co.
                  P.O. Box 596
                  Liberal, KS 67905-0596
                  www.1solalliance.com

Disclaimer & Legal Notice

The information contained in this book is intended to be educational and not for diagnosis, prescription, or treatment of any health disorder whatsoever. This information should not replace consultation with a competent healthcare professional. The content of the book is intended to be used as an adjunct to a rational and responsible healthcare program prescribed by a licensed healthcare practitioner. This is a book about faith. As such the author and publisher do not warrant the success any person would have using any of the exercises and techniques contained herein. Success and failure will vary. The author and publisher therefore are in no way liable for any misuse of the material contained herein.

To protect the identity and privacy of others, most of the names within this book have been adapted, modified and changed for confidentiality purposes. Any resemblance to real persons, living or dead is purely coincidental.

Cover art, illustrations and photographs by: Derric "Rau Khu" Moore
Stock photos courtesy of Dreamstine.com

ISBN: 978-0-9855067-4-2

Printed in the United States of America

MAA AANKH

Volume III

The Kamitic Shaman Way of Working the
Superconscious Mind to Improve Memory,
Solve Problems Intuitively and Spiritually
Grow Through the Power of the Spirits

Other Books by the Author:

MAA AANKH Volume I:

Finding God the Afro-American Spiritual Way,

by Honoring the Ancestors and Guardian Spirits

Kamta: A Practical Kamitic Path for Obtaining Power

Maa: A Guide to the Kamitic Way for Personal Transformation

MAA AANKH Volume II:

Discovering the Power of I AM Using the Shamanic Principles of

Ancient Egypt for Self-Empowerment and Personal Development

Honoring the Ancestors the Kemetic Shaman Way:

A Practical Manual for Venerating and Working with the Ancestors

from a God Perspective

The Kamta Primer: A Practical Shamanic Guide for Using Kemetic

Ritual, Magick and Spirituality for Acquiring Power

En Español: Maa Aankh Volume I:

Encontrando a Dios al Modo Espiritual Afroamericano, Honrando a

los Ancestros y a los Espíritus Guardianes

CONTENTS

LIST OF FIGURES

MAA AANKH
Volume III

The Kamitic Shaman Way of Working the
Superconscious Mind to Improve Memory,
Solve Problems Intuitively and Spiritually
Grow Through the Power of the Spirits

And when he was demanded of the Pharisees, when the kingdom of God should come, he answered them and said, The kingdom of God cometh not with observation: Neither shall they say, Lo here! or, lo there! for, behold, the kingdom of God is within you.

– Luke17: 20 – 21, KJV

Introduction:
What is Kamitic Shamanism?

I have always been fascinated with the traditions of other cultures, but after studying various faiths, traditions and the history of classic cultures (particularly the ancient Egyptians) for some time now. What I discovered was that everyone does magic because telling our self to do something versus actually doing it, are two completely different things. This is the reason we all have our favorite colognes, perfumes, favorite colors, favorite pieces of jewelry, etc. that we use to influence the world around us. For instance, whenever we want to create a loving, romantic mood, many of us will burn soft colored pink, yellow or even white candles and sweet smelling incense, while playing seductive or sultry music. When preparing for a job interview, most of us will wear dark colored attire, to give the impression that we are conservative, responsible and powerful individuals that can be trusted to get the job done. We all use these symbols in order to influence the people around us to accept us, appreciate us, bless us, assist us, protect us, and love us, and this in essence is what magic is all about.

What this means is that most of us do magic unconsciously. For instance, while walking through a park we might see a small stone and decide to pick it up for no apparent reason, and on our way home avoid an accident. We may get a hunch to take a different route to a location we frequently visit and encounter a new love. The reason we all do magic is because it is our birthright that was passed on to us by our most ancient of ancestors. And even though many of us may not publicly acknowledge that we perform some type of magical rite in our life. We all do magic because magic enhances our likelihood of certain outcomes over others. It basically stacks the cards in our favor. If the chances of us getting a date with a particular celebrity were 1 out of 100, then magic would increases our odds by making them 1 out of 50, 25 or even 5 depending upon the circumstances.

So, we see from this perspective magic works and it works all the time because its true purpose is to increase an individual's chances of success. From a psychological perspective, we know that our chances of success have increased whenever we witness phenomenal events, which Swiss psychiatrist Carl Gustav Jung calls "synchronicity."

What is Synchronicity?

In Jung's book *Memories, Dreams, Reflections,* he defines synchronicity as a set of meaningful coincidence of a physical or psychic (such as a dream, fantasy, or thought), which has no causal relationship to one another. These events coincide in time in a way that gives meaning to the observer such as a premonition coming true, or an image from a dream, idea, thought, etc. occurring at the same time in a different place. Synchronistic events according to Jung, occur where neither one nor the other, coincidence can be explained intellectually by causality. Their inexplicability is not due to the fact that the cause is unknown but can't be explain using scientific logic.

For instance, Jung noted that a synchronicity existed between the life of Christ, and an astronomical event marking the beginning of the spring equinox with the sign Pisces, which explained the reason why Christ is seen in Christendom as the leader of a new age. Jung even tells how he witnessed a synchronistic event in his life. He explains how while he was having a dream he dreamt of an old man with horns carrying four keys, one which he was using to open a lock. He also had the wing of a kingfisher, which is a brightly colored bird. Jung stated that he didn't understand his dream so to help him to memorize it, he painted it. A few days later he said he found a dead kingfisher that was lying in his garden, which was unusual since it was rare to find this brightly colored bird in Zurich. Further examination revealed that the bird had been dead for a few days but showed no sign of external injury. It was this acausal event that convinced him the kingfisher was a sign from his dreams and led him to see the old man in his as his personal archetype, which he later called Philemon. Although Jung did not believe that Philemon sent the kingfisher, thus causing the synchronistic event to occur. He believed that synchronistic events occur whenever an archetype enters into our consciousness.

Jung borrowed the word archetype from Plato who was trying to understand what is "real" and what is "constant". Plato noticed that when he relied solely upon his five senses, as we do today, that they could easily be misled because there is a reality that is bound by time and space, and another that is not. For instance, if we look at a dog and let say this dog's name is Spot, what we are seeing is a biological creature that at some point will die. Yet, the dog has characteristics that distinguish it from other dogs. If the dog were allowed to reproduce, it would pass on to its offspring, these same unique characteristics that again would distinguish it from other dogs in its species. This means that there is a part of the dog that will not die, which Plato called a form, because as long as there are dogs that exist. This unique characteristic will continue to be passed on to Spot's offspring. The real Spot is immortal part of the dog that does not die and it is what makes up Spot's instincts or intuition.

Plato realized what many are beginning to comprehend, is that our life is an illusion. What many of us are calling reality is not real. Yes, physically it exists but it is a reflection of something much more profound. The part of us that most of us identify with is what Jung calls the ego. The ego thinks it is in charge only because it can manipulate physical events but it doesn't have any intuition. This is the reason magical and miraculous events fascinate us, because they exist outside of our ego's physical reach.

When Jung decided to explore the unconscious mind at the deepest levels that is where he found Plato's forms or his psychic patterns /personalities that he called archetypes, which could be found all throughout the world in various myths and religions. At the deepest level he found that these archetypes – that people have called for ages, gods, goddesses, demons, spirits, saints, etc. – seemed to have merged into a collective unconscious, but by using symbols they could be called back into one's awareness. **<u>So whenever we perform magic, technically what we are doing is using symbols to manipulate our psyche,</u>** which brings back into our awareness an archetypal pattern, thus resulting in a magical event or synchronicity. In other words, when you burn an incense and candle to create a loving mood, put on the dark suit or dress for a job interview, etc. and you are successful in doing what you want. You are invoking the spirit or goddess of love, thus doing magic because you have created a synchronicity by using symbols.

So, what this means is that what we call magic and miracles in contemporary times is anything that occurs unexpectedly in relation to our goals and wishes. For example, if a person's prayer for full recovery of an illness has their prayer answered. They would call it a miracle while another might call it magic, but psychologically speaking the individual was simply creating a host of synchronicities. Therefore, a set of synchronicities practiced amongst a particular culture is what people would commonly call folk practices or a folk religion by people outside of that cultural experience. The adherents on the other hand would call this system of synchronicities a cultural traditions, which is a host of beliefs, practices and/or rituals passed down within a particular group with a special or symbolic meaning connecting them with their ancestral past.

Therefore, everyone does magic because the purpose of magic is to influence one's immediate environment by increasing one's odds in being successful in accomplishing their will. If you wish, pray, hope, etc. to be successful in any endeavor and combine this intention with any symbol, you are doing some form of magic to express your will symbolically. If you learned a systematic way of doing this from you're a loved one, friend or some other member of your family, community, etc. then you are engaging in a folk practice or cultural tradition.

My Santeria Experience

I learned about cultural traditions while living in Florida. In fact, it was synchronicity (my interests in cultural traditions particularly those derived from Africa) that led me to meet Papa, a little black man who migrated from Cuba. Prior to meeting Papa, I had read and studied books on history, mysticism, science, religion, metaphysics, art and African philosophy and spirituality, in hopes of becoming more spiritual. After meeting Papa, I realized that books were guides that were full of theories. This is because Papa who was a *babalawo* (high priest in the Santeria religion) and a member of the all-male *Abakua* society, helped me to see that all of my research and studying only enhanced my intellect, thus making me a great debater in metaphysics, but my studies didn't do anything for me spiritually.

In the short time that I knew Papa, we talked about everything under the sun. One of the things that interested me the most about Papa was what he called *la manera (my way in Spanish),* which he explained was his own particular way of connecting with God. Papa said that it was because of his *la manera,* that he didn't have to read books, he didn't have to follow what other people told him to do, etc. All he needed to do was listen to the inner voice speaking within him, because it guided him perfectly.

I didn't really understand at the time all of what Papa was telling me, but everything he told me. I wrote in my *el libro* (journal used in Santeria). Occasionally, I would reflect back upon the stories and proverbs he told. One of the things he mentioned to me after seeing how interested I was in learning from him was how happy he was to see that African Americans had schools, businesses, organizations, churches, etc. The thing that upset him was that he found that many African Americans didn't have a cultural tradition, which he discovered was due to cultural terrorism, particularly by groups like the Ku Klux Klan. It was this realization that led Papa to scold me so that I did not mimic others, and encourage me to investigate my own tradition.

Some, time after meeting Papa I began having a lot of problems. That's when I met an Oshun priestess (who was first initiated into Santeria and later into the Yoruba religion in Nigeria), whom I called Iya (Yoruba for mother). Iya who was a gifted diviner picked up on my connection with Egypt and told me that the reason I was having so many problems in my life was because I was called to be a shaman. Upon hearing the news, I rejected it because in my mind the life of a shaman was difficult. When I finally accepted it I noticed that there was no information on Egyptian shamanism. In fact, the terms Egyptian and shamanism were rarely even joined together. Then one day I came across James Hall's

Sangoma: My Odyssey Into the Spirit World of Africa, which gave me a better picture of the role that shamans play particularly in South Africa. This made me realize that the first Africans brought to North America tried to recreate and rebuild their cultural tradition by following a shamanic path, which inspired me to learn about the spiritual plight of African Americans.

African American Mysticism & Sacred Science

When the Africans were kidnapped, enslaved and taken to the Americas. These brave souls in the Americas had to recreate their cultural traditions in the New World. Those Africans taken to the Caribbean and South America were able to recreate their cultural traditions by masking the concepts and principles under the Catholic guise. As a result, those taken to Brazil managed to successfully create Candomble, Quibanda and Macuumba. The Africans taken to Haiti created Vodun, while those taken to Cuba created Lucumi (Santeria) and Palo Mayombe, but the Africans taken to North America did not have the same fate.

The enslavers in North America were mostly Protestants, which made it nearly impossible for the Africans to disguise their beliefs and masks their African concepts and principles. The lack of a similar religious structure combined with the ceasing of the importation of slaves from Africa and surrounding areas, created an African theological deficit, which forced the Africans taken to North America (and other British controlled territories) to rely solely upon the ancestral memories, and the influences they encountered in their new homeland. In North America, the Africans taken there created what some call a new Afro – Atlantic religion. In John Thornton's book, *Africa and Africans in the Making of the Atlantic World, 1400 – 1800,* Thornton writes that the Africans didn't just accept the belief system of their oppressors. The Africans analyzed, evaluated, borrowed and blended various ideas and concepts to address their immediate needs. This religious syncretism Thornton states, occurred mainly in the interpretation and revelation of the spirit world in which both the African and Europeans believed. Thornton states that:

> African revelation in the sixteenth and seventeenth centuries can be divided into several categories. Augury and divination involved the study of events to determine other – worldly intentions. Dream interpretation relies on the notion that other world can sometimes communicate with the unconscious mind. More dramatic revelations came in the form of visions, or hearing voices, usually only be people with special gifts. Perhaps the most dramatic form of revelation was given through spirit medium or possessed object, in which an other – worldly entity took over a human, animal or material object and spoke through it.

In other words, the Africans because of their "other worldly" beliefs and experiences, Africanized Christianity by introducing to Protestant Christianity numerous African spiritual practices such as shouting, speaking in tongues, dancing in the spirit, spirit possession, being slain in the spirit, visions, and prophecies (channeling), all of which have been embraced and integrated in some form into most American churches especially the Pentecostal denominations.

A history of American Christianity will reveal that none of these influences existed prior to the Azusa Street Revival of 1906, which consisted of a number of attendees (blacks, whites, Hispanics and Asians from various social classes during the Jim Crow era), who spoke in tongues or were occasionally slain by the spirit, because Europeans although they believed in the existence of heaven, saw this as being works of the devil. If it had not been for the leader of this historic event, William J. Seymour, the one – eyed son of a former slave and student of Pentecostal preacher Charles Parham, American churches would not be as vibrant and charismatic as they are known today. Unbeknown to most is that when Parham, Seymour's mentor first witnessed the Azusa Street Revival, he disassociated himself from it and disregarded it as a hoax performed by ignorant mesmerizers and spiritualists. Consequently, the Azusa Street Revival gave birth to the Pentecostal movement.

I learned that few people are aware of the strong African spiritual influence in American history because most people don't have a clue about African American culture except for the stereotypical images that are commonly portrayed by the media. This is mainly because, African Americans like the Native Americans, have been constant victims of cultural appropriation.

Cultural appropriation according to Susan Safidi, author of *Who Owns Culture? Appropriation and Authenticity in American Law* is defined as "Taking intellectual property, traditional knowledge, cultural expressions, or artifacts from someone else's culture without permission." Further explained "This can include unauthorized use of another culture's dance, dress, music, language, folklore, cuisine, traditional medicine, religious symbols, etc. It's most likely to be harmful when the source community is a minority group that has been oppressed or exploited in other ways or when the object of appropriation is particularly sensitive, e.g. sacred objects." For example, the Native American use of stones, herbs for smudging, attire, etc. is a prime example of cultural appropriation. Another example, can be found in the use of the popular word "mojo" which, was a term describing an African American amulet that has been denoted to meaning one's sexual prowess.

Cultural appropriation in short is a colonialist mentality where the dominant culture simply says, "I'll take that!" and uses whatever it has taken from the minority group for its own selfish purpose. It is harmful for a few reasons:

1. The first being, it is an insult to the memory of those individuals that worked hard to preserve the tradition, so that their descendants could survive persecution.

2. It is harmful because when a minority group has had everything taken from them (e.g. name, language, families, land, etc.) by a dominant culture, except for their tradition. The dominant culture, unconcerned about the purpose of the tradition, will objectify the oppressed group's practices, thus making it to be viewed by the public as being either a fad or an object that can be purchased for the right price.

3. Third, it gives the dominant culture a false sense that they have the right to adapt, change and modify minority traditions to suit their will and pass it on as being authentic. While the minority group's tradition is viewed as being unauthentic.

4. Lastly, it encourages disparity amongst minorities while promoting stereotypes because it makes the assumption that all minority groups are the same and have had the same experiences.

This is the reason, nothing substantial has been written on African American cultural traditions. As a result, African American mysticism is never expressed in the church because the dominant culture in the past disregarded it as "Negro superstition" and not a serious spiritual way of life, which "they" called hoodoo.

It is interesting that when I looked up the word hoodoo, it is classified as a noun (as in a practice), a transitive verb (such as "I hoodoo you") or an adjective (to describe a practitioner like a hoodoo man), and that it was first documented in American English in 1875. Yet most African American families never used the term. In fact, most African Americans only heard of the term after coming in contact with whites. It is only then that they realize that what they are referring to as hoodoo is African American cultural traditions. Even more interesting is that no one even knows the origin of the term. However, Eoghan Ballard, a folklorist and ethnologist specializing in Afro – Caribbean traditions, theorizes after comparing the cultural practices of early African Americans with the surviving Kongolese traditions of Cuba. That the word hoodoo is most like a corruption of the Spanish word "Judio" pronounced "hoo-dee-oh" meaning Jewish. In other words, Ballard believes that the New World Spaniards used the term to signify the Africans that refused to relinquish their cultural beliefs, customs and practices and become "good (obedient, passive, and docile)" Christian slaves. This means that the word hoodoo is a derogatory term that was most likely used to define African American cultural traditions.

Several years later, after meeting with Papa and Iya, I became deathly ill and was diagnosed with having lupus. Around the same time, that is when I learned that my mother, grandmother, aunts and uncles would use blessed olive oil for protection, healing and blessings. When I would bring the subject up and ask how come they never told me about it. The subject was always ignored. That's when I learned that the reason most African Americans who were descendants of individuals outside of Louisiana, learned not to talk about hoodoo was because the term was synonymous with witchcraft. But whites couldn't distinguish between spiritual practices and witchcraft. In response they branded all African derived traditions as being evil. This is why most African Americans outside of Louisiana, never used the term hoodoo to describe their spirituality.

To understand why the early African Americans did this we have to realize that when the first Europeans and their descendants accused other whites of witchcraft. These people were simply given a trial, imprisoned, and persecuted and if found guilty burned as was the case of the Salem witch trials. Early African Americans who were not even seen as human beings were simply persecuted and lynched by suspecting and angry white mobs. It became apparent that the reason the term hoodoo was not used was because early African Americans taught their descendants how to maintain and preserve their tradition, by adhering to a strict code of secrecy and camouflaging their beliefs under the guise of Protestant Christianity. It is for this reason, the collection of folklore collected by Anglican minister Harry Middleton Hyatt and published in his book *Hoodoo--Conjuration--Witchcraft—Rootwork*, most likely is probably less than fifty percent accurate because black people being very communal during this period would not divulge any information about themselves or practice unless the individual was family. This is not to say that Hyatt's work is fraudulent but, he was viewed as an outsider in their community and would have been treated as such for defensive reasons.

So, with no saints to venerate like the Africans in Cuba, Brazil and Haiti, and African mysticism not being publicly expressed in the church, every phenomenon was attributed to God, while the Biblical characters that acted as conduits for God's Power for the Children of Israel, became the new cosmic archetypes for the enslaved Africans and their descendants. This is how they were able to continue this secret tradition.

Now, I tried to understand how this unique tradition first evolved because as I had mentioned. I was always fascinated with the subject, but when I became ill. I felt like part of my remedy in overcoming this disease was to understand, organize, outline and implement my ancestors' mystical sciences and sacred tradition for myself and loved ones.

Through research I discovered that contrary to popular belief, the first Africans brought to North America (and the Americas in general) were from the Kongo Angolan region, because these were the first Africans that Portuguese explorers encountered. As always the case when a more technologically advanced culture encounters a less technologically advanced culture. When the Kongo people met these Europeans, they were so impressed by them that the Kongo king willingly converted to Christianity around 1485 and declared the Kongo kingdom a Christian state. From that time on, some Kongo priesthood members and Portuguese missionaries worked to create a practical religious syncretism. The syncretism between the two cultures was simplified because the Kongo religion did not consist of a pantheon of divinities like the other Africans (Akans, Yoruba, Fons, etc.) in neighboring countries. The people of the Kongo believed in one God whom they called Nzambi Mpungu – the Supreme God – and several classes of spirits that existed under the Divine called the basimbi (benevolent spirits very similar to martyrs and saints), bankuyu (malevolent spirits similar to devils and imps) and the most important spirits of all, the bakulu (ancestral spirits and the elders who were near death – associated with Luvemba – the setting sun in the Kongo Cross shown below).

The bakulu were greatly honored, respected and feared because it was believed the spirits of the dead could influence the life of the living. Since the ancestral spirits were intimately tied to the land of dead also called the land of the ancestors, and when an elder died they took their wisdom with them to the mysterious land of the ancestors. The land of the ancestors was believed to be pure and full of whiteness. For this reason, white or greying hair was seen as a sign in the Old Kongo, that one was either touched by an ancestor or had spiritually travelled to the kingdom of the ancestors or the kingdom of whiteness and had obtained spiritual wisdom to help themselves and others in the natural world. Speaking of whiteness, when a just decision was made by a tribunal, it was believed that the lawsuit. Through the just decision caused the victor to be reborn because those on the tribunal had retrieved ancestral wisdom. The individual on some occasions was anointed with white clay because they had been purified from the shame, disgrace, etc. of the lawsuit.

For this reason, elders were associated with the setting sun, which was also symbolized as the color white. All elders (especially older men for their male aggressiveness) were greatly honored and respected because they were seen as walking conduits who were preparing to go to the other side (to die). So, the last thing anyone wanted to do was send an elder to the kingdom of the ancestral whiteness with a bad report of what some living descendant had done.

This was the basis of the Old Kongo religion, so when they converted to Christianity. These same spirits in the Old Kongo were easily syncretized and the basimbi became Christian angels and saints. The bankuyu were associated with devils and demonic spirits, while the bakulu became Christian martyrs. Jesus Christ quickly became an ancestral spirit associated with the ancestral kingdom of whiteness.

Although the Kongo people didn't have a large pantheon of spirits like the Akan, Yoruba and Fons, they did however have a pantheon of spiritual charms that harnessed the power of the spirits called nkisi (spiritual medicine). The nkisi were spiritual agents or spiritual tools created for specific tasks like "to improve health over fever, epilepsy, impotency, fertility" or "protect one homes from fire, burglary, civil discord", etc. Many of the nkisi or bankisi (plural) were composed of objects symbolizing the ancestral kingdom of whiteness, which included seashells, bones, white stones (especially quartz crystals and white stones), white clay, last used objects, etc.). The belief was that since the ancestors had become pure, enlightened and wise beings, that they would empower the spiritual medicine to fulfill the specific task.

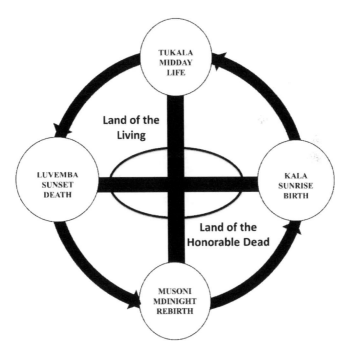

Figure 1: Bantu-Kongo Yowa, Dikenga or Kongo Cross

The spiritual foundation of the Old Kongo religion, however centered on a unique cosmogram called Yowa Cross, Dikenga, Tendwa Kia Nza-n Kongo or simply the Kongo Cross. According to the late Dr. Kimbwandende Kia Bunseki Fu-Kiau the Kongo Cross didn't just provide a philosophical understanding of the universe, but it provided an alchemical, metaphysical, psychological and esoteric understanding as well because it permeated every aspect of the Kongo culture.

The general understanding of the cosmogram is that Nzambi – the Supreme Being – is imagined as being above and the honorable dead are seen as being below. The horizontal line called *kalunga,* symbolizing a body of water, separates the kingdom of the living above, from the kingdom of the dead or kingdom of whiteness. Surrounding both kingdoms was four discs at the end of each arm symbolize the four moments of the sun – sunrise, midday, sunset and midnight.

The disc symbolizing sunrise called Kala was black because everything from soil, to buds, etc. was black in color. The midday sun was called Tukula the color red representing male aggressiveness and young women menstrual, thus signifying the moment of adulthood. Sunset was called Luvemba the color white since when things died all that remained were bones, white ash, etc. thus, indicating that the fire of life had been extinguished. Midnight (when the sun was believed to be on the other side) was called Musoni and is the color yellow (old or aged whites), thus the color of rebirth.

Man's and woman's soul mirrors the moments of the sun as – birth, life, death and rebirth. It signified that man's soul does not die, but like the sun it will either be reborn through one's progeny or in some other form in nature. Thus the righteous will not be destroyed but will have everlasting life, by either becoming a higher spirit or reincarnating into a progeny.

When Christian missionaries syncretized the crucifix with the Kongo Cross and the Old Kongo religion, the Kongo most likely didn't see it as symbolizing the crucifixion of the Christian savior. Most likely what they saw was that the life and death of Jesus actually confirmed what they already believed. Jesus therefore became a visible symbol or an archetype for the righteous and proof of the continuity of the soul. Therefore, when the first Africans from the Kongo – Angolan region, arrived on the shores of North America in late August 1619, they were either Africanized Christians or already had some practical knowledge of the Christian faith. These Kongo descendants brought with them and used the Kongo Cross as a guide, which art historian Robert Farris Thompson described in his books, *The Four Moments of the Sun: Kongo Art in Two Worlds* as:

> "Coded as a cross, a quartered circle or diamond, a seashell spiral, or a special cross with solar emblems at each ending - the sign of the four moments of the sun is the Kongo emblem of spiritual continuity and renaissance par excellence. In certain rites it is written on the earth, and a person stands upon it to take an oath, or to signify that he or she understands the meaning of life as a process shared with the dead below the river or the sea - **the real sources of earthly power and prestige, in Kongo thinking...** (Emphasis mine) The intimation, by shorthand geometric statements, of mirrored worlds within the spiritual journey of the sun, is the source and illumination of some of the more important sculptural gestures and decorative signs pertaining to funerary monuments and objects designated for deposit on the surface of funerary tombs, or otherwise connected with funerary ceremonies and the end of life."

Consequently, traces of the cross have been found all throughout the New World, and in North America it has been found inscribed on colonoware amongst slave quarters. It is remnant of the old African American ring shout. Old African gravesites have been found with a host of white seashells or painted pottery expressing the Old Kongo Cross and continuity of the soul. A variation of the original Kongo Cross was found at the First African Baptist Church in Savanah Georgia, which according to historians was used as a marker to assist fleeing slaves on the Underground Railroad.

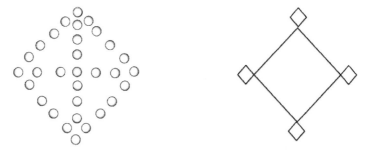

Figure 2: Sketch of Kongo Cross, Savannah GA (l)
Figure 3: Diamond Shape Cosmograms Found throughout the South (r)

This means that along with an Africanized Christianity, the Africans from the Kongo Angolan region also brought with them their small pantheon, especially their ancestral spirits. So the bakulu (ancestral spirits and the association with the ancestral kingdom of whiteness) from the Old Kongo became in Protestant North America the Fathers and Mothers of the Church who to this day are often depicted wearing white (silver, grey or some light colored attire).

Today African American ancestors are venerated by having rooms, church pews, etc. named in their honor. Many African Americans also keep the last items used by their beloved dead such as plants, bibles and other last used objects, which is a remnant of the Old Kongo nkisi practice. Also, during special occasions, white flowers are worn in memory of a departed loved one. Most African American churches also venerate their ancestors by displaying an image of these individuals in the main hallway or some other prominent area leading to the main sanctuary of the church. In most African American homes they also venerate their ancestors by having a photo or portrait of the departed loved one, which coincidentally is usually, situated facing the west (the setting sun direction) proof of an ancestral memory.

The basimbi (the benevolent spirits similar to martyrs and saints) manifested themselves mainly as Christian archetypes. The most famous basimbi spirit is the biblical Moses who has inspired numerous movements throughout North America. It is a known fact that heroes and heroines such as Harriet Tubman all the way to Martin L. King Jr. were all inspired by Moses, but there were others.

Even the Kongo bankuyu (the malevolent spirits similar to devils and imps) survived in North America. The famous adventures of Brer Rabbit are believed to be by some the inspiration behind the popular cartoon character Bugs Bunny. Other bankuyu survived as haunts or ghosts and as the *blues* of Blues music, which are not seen as being necessarily evil as in the Christian sense, but mischievous spirits that brings one down. Note if you will how all of these forms are anthropomorphized e.g. the *blues* came by my door.

All of this made me want to learn more about the Kongo faith, but unfortunately because the people of the Kongo – Angolan region were the first the European encountered. They were also the most devastated by slavery, imperialism, civil war, corruption, etc. This made learning about an unadulterated version of the Kongo philosophies virtually impossible, but, in the course of my research, an alternative presented itself.

One day while observing my grandmother's obituary I noticed that above her birth date was written "Sunrise" and the day of her passing was the word "Sunset," which associated her life with the sun. I had never noticed this before, but went I viewed other obituaries; I saw that this format was common mainly amongst African Americans. This clearly led me to realize that there was a Kongo influence in my family. I remembered that my grandparents' home was also full of diamond cosmogram imagery, like Dr. Farris had mentioned in his books. Then that's when it happened, I got the notion to look at the *Story of Ra and Oset (Isis)*.

In the *Story*, Oset poisons the sun – god Ra in order to trick him into revealing his name, so that she can freely use his power at will. When Ra becomes deathly ill, he calls upon all of his children to help him but only Oset is able to do so. She tells Ra that in order for her to drive the poison from his, she needs his real name and Ra responds to her saying:

> *"I have made the heavens and the earth, I have ordered the mountains, I have created all that is above them, I have made the water, I have made to come into being the great and wide sea, I have made the 'Bull of his mother,' from whom spring the delights of love. I have made the heavens, I have stretched out the two horizons like a curtain, and I have placed the soul of the gods within them. I am he who, if he openeth his eyes, doth make the light, and, if he closeth them, darkness cometh into being. At his command the Nile riseth, and the gods know not his name. I have made the hours, I have created the days, I bring forward the festivals of the year, I create the Nile-flood. I make the fire of life, and I provide food in the*

houses. I am Khepera in the morning, I am Ra at noon, and I am Tmu at evening."

It was the last stanza of Ra's response *"I am Khepera in the morning, I am Ra at noon, and I am Tmu at evening."* that made me see that he was not an actual deity, but he symbolized the Spirit of God or God's Divine Power. When I compared the names that Ra gave to Oset, they correlated almost perfectly. For instance, Khepera was associated with the sunrise and was described as a black or dark greenish scarab beetle. Ra was associated with the midday sun and was often depicted as being red like fire. Tmu also called Ra Atum was associated with the evening sun and the dead kings in the West – particularly Osar (Asar, Ausar or Osiris) who is always depicted as a mummy wearing white bandages, and. Amun Ra the Hidden Ra was always depicted as a young man wearing golden yellow plumes – the same color as Musoni.

It was too good to be true and still to this day, the uncanniness of it all still makes my hair stand up on my neck. In any case, this is when I had no choice but to surrender my ego and acknowledge that there was definitely an ancestral presence that was guiding me through this whole process. That's when I was instructed to call to connect the dots and call the cosmogram below the Maa Aankh.

The basic interpretation of the Maa Aankh is that it symbolizes our universe and illustrates that there are two realities – a visible, physical realm above called TASETT – The Red Lands (red being the color of life, heat, activity, etc.) is ruled by Set, symbolized by the red crown. And, the hidden and invisible spiritual realm below called KAMTA – The Black Lands (black being the color of mystery, the unknown, power, etc.) which is governed by the Lord of the Ancestors symbolized by the white crown.

xxi

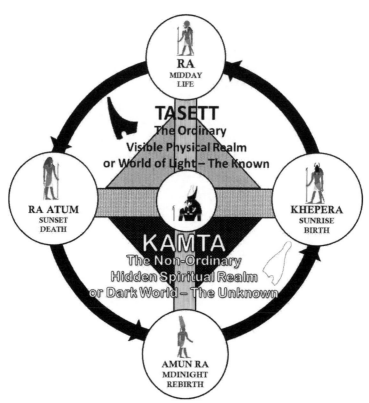

Figure 4: Maa Aankh Cosmogram

These two realities are separated metaphorically by a chaotic body of water called nyun, but they are united by the vertical line called the Maa, thus making the popular Kamitic axiom, "As above, so below" true. The solar disc surrounding the Maa Aankh symbolize the four moments of the sun – Khepera (sunrise/black), Ra (midday/red), Ra Atum (sunset/white) and Amun Ra (midnight/yellow). Our soul therefore mirrors the movement of the sun (birth, life, death and rebirth).

Thereby revealing that our soul is immortal and that the righteous will not die but will be reborn spiritually, mentally and physically. Righteousness signifies that like the sun, one's soul has journey through the harsh realities of the physical realm and passed through the realm of the spirit in order to become whole. In other words, we like the sun die and are reborn every day.

Finding the Truth, the Way, the Maa

I must admit that when I first discovered the Maa Aankh, I was a little apprehensive on writing about it, because I knew that there was no cosmogram like it that had been found in Ancient Egypt. Not only that, even though a lot of research had been done tying the ancient Egyptians to Sub Sahara Africa. I was afraid that most people would see the whole thing as being a fraud or some made up system created to give people a false sense of self and pride. Then I found that Sir E. A. Wallis Budge's in his book, *Osiris: The Egyptian Religion of Resurrection* listed numerous examples, which verified that the ancient Egyptians and many of the people of Sub – Sahara Africa were in fact kin to one another based upon cultural similarities. Some of the facts that Budge discovered were:

- The moon rather than the sun was associated with the Supreme Being, a fact that was verified by the Maa Aankh, because the moon is associated with Amun Ra, the highest and most unadulterated attribute of the Divine.

- The uncanny widespread practice of giving birth in the bush resembles Isis (Aset, Auset, Oset) giving birth to Horus (Heru, Hru) in the swamp. On the Maa Aankh, the bush and the swamp symbolize KAMTA the land of the spiritual realm and mysteries.

- The beetle and the frog symbolize new life in ancient Egypt and Sub – Sahara Africa. Again, Khepera represents sunrise and a new beginning.

There were a host of other similarities that Budge listed, which verified to me that the Maa Aankh was channeled to me from a legitimate ancestral source. The time had come now for me to work it in order to get a better understand of it, in order to overcome this lupus illness, so I did just that.

From Kemet to Kamit and the Akhenaten & Moses Mystery

As I worked with the Maa Aankh, I got a better understanding of both the ancient Egyptians and my ancestors as they dwelled in the Americas. For instance, I had learned prior to my discovery that the ancient Egyptians called their country according to archeological and historical research KMT, which most have interpreted, translated and pronounced as Kemetic – meaning "the Black Lands." The term is a pun based on the dark soil in the southern region due to the inundation of the Nile. As a result, most people prefer to use the word Kemetic instead of ancient Egypt because the latter is derived from the Greek word Aegiptos, and to stress importance on the Pharoanic or dynastic time period prior to the Greek rule around 332 BC. Generally speaking all the Kemetic traditions are referred to as Kemeticism.

Many of the individuals following the Kemetic path are very interested in the ancient Egyptian mysteries and the Kemetic initiation systems. Some have even gone so far as to celebrate the Kemetic holidays, rites, rituals and the whole Kemetic way of life. I will not lie. I used to be very interested in this as well, but when Papa scolded me for mimicking a dead culture. The lesson stayed with me because he told me that it was foolish to mimic what they did thousands of years ago. I remember him saying that what worked during their time, worked specifically for that ancient time period. I recall on one occasion him telling me that this was the reason the African elders, when they arrived in Cuba, had to syncretize the orisha with the Catholic saints in order to fight the cruelty of slavery. He told me instead of mimicking that I needed to focus on the concepts and principles because he said that the concepts and principles will never change. The reason they will never change, Papa said, was because traditional African religions and diaspora practices stem from the same root. Santeria, like all of the other traditions, was just a branch from the same tree.

I always reflected back to this time when Papa reprimanded me, but I am grateful that he did. It was because of him that I focused only on the concepts and principles, which helped me to discover the Maa Aankh. Now, after studying the Maa Aankh for some time, I arrived at a more profound and esoteric understanding of the term KMT, which revealed that the reason the ancients referred to their origins as "the Black Lands" because they were also alluding to the belief that they came from the spiritual realm or the Land of Nothingness – the mysterious Spirit Realm. This same concept exists in numerous Sub Saharan African cosmologies particularly the Kongo philosophy. Most Kemetic groups and organizations I noticed miss this point because they focus only on the Kemetic religion, which forces them to see Osiris as a Jesus Christ equivalent. This makes Osiris' brother Set (Seth or Typhon in Greek) the devil, which creates the whole Western good versus evil concept. This basically in my opinion degenerates into another form of dogma, just replacing the savior of one religion with another. Everything from this perspective is categorized as being either good or evil, because it is based upon western thinking. This is why I rarely found any of these Kemetic groups talking about magical practices because from a western perspective magic is divided into good and evil or so – called white (or high magic) and black (low and dark) magic.

The Kemetic people didn't think like this. They didn't believe that Osiris was the epitome of good and Set the epitome of evil. Good and evil was all relative to one's situation. This is why they didn't have any commandments telling people dogmatically "Thou shalt not kill," because such a commandment would be inapplicable if an individual was forced to defend his or her family or protect his or her nation during war times. This is why I had to look beyond the dogma.

When I continued to look beyond the religious aspect and ignored the Western concept of good and evil. I found that Osiris was most likely modeled after the legendary king Narmer also known as Menes, the first ruler to unite the divided country into one. This means that these beliefs, ideas and concepts existed in pre – dynastic times from a much older civilization than Kemet, hence an Ancient Egyptian shamanism. Osiris was therefore Narmer deified, which makes him actually a deified ancestor. Since King Narmer was said to have come from the southern region of the country – esoterically speaking the spirit realm or the kingdom of the ancestors. This meant that all of the so – called gods and goddesses of Kemet were all once upon a time living people who were immortalized into archetypical ancestors. In other words, if Osiris is not the epitome of good and Set is not the epitome of evil, but actual ancestors. They symbolized polar opposites from an ancient African perspective, which explains why Set on numerous occasions was portrayed as a hero in the ancient legends in order to bring about balance.

I found cultural proof that Osiris was a deified ancestor in various stories about him especially in the relationship between him and his son Horus. For instance, in the legendary story after Horus defeats his uncle in a civil court of law, he is awarded his father's white crown, thus symbolizing the unification of the country. In the classic Kongo culture, when an individual won a lawsuit, they were anointed with white chalk, white symbolizing the land of the ancestors or in ancient Egypt the land of Osiris. Today throughout the Afro – diaspora when an individual is said to have gone to the other side (especially in the case of spirit possession) they are anointed with white chalk. This cultural practice was extended to American churches, which is why individuals were baptized in white gowns.

When I compared these cultural similarities with the cultural practices the Africans brought to North America, I found that because the Protestant enslavers would not let the Africans worship in their native language or in their own manner alone out of fear of a revolt. The Africans would stole away into the fields or have their own religious services in the bush, which is where the ancestors and spirits dwelled.

This was all new and insightful information that painted an entirely different perspective about the ancient Egyptians. To reflect the ancient African shamanic perspective, that is pre – dynastic era, Osiris became Osar (Asar, Ausar), because he is viewed as ancient ancestor. I chose the term Kamit and this particular branch of Kemeticism became what I call Kamitic Shamanism.

So What about Akhenaten and Moses?

Kamitic Shamanism helped me in a number of ways. One of the things it helped me to do was correct the distorted view I had about the Kamitic people due to my religious upbringing and Cecile B. DeMille's *Ten Commandments*.

Like many who were fascinated with the Kamitic traditions, I had learned about the Kamitic king Akhenaten. I even for a brief moment entertained the idea of following Akhenaten's path because he was said to be the father of monotheism, since he founded the religion historians refer to as Atenism. Usually archeologists report that when Akhenaten first introduced his new faith Atenism to the Kamitic people. They rejected in favor of their pagan ways. As a result, the Bible paints the picture that the Kamitic people preferred to be heathens, while the Quran goes so far as to say that they worshipped Satan. All of this I began to see was an attempt to legitimize the whole *Exodus* story. The same holds true for those scholars that claimed that Akhenaten was either the biblical Moses or that Moses was a follower of Akhenaten's religious cult. The main reason these theories continue to persist is because:

1. Most are under the impression that the biblical account of the Exodus was a factual and historical event, despite the fact that the bible doesn't mention the ruling king during the time of the *Exodus*, doesn't give any other evidence verifying when the thousands of people allegedly fled ancient Egypt, and.

2. The second reason is because there is historical proof that the ancient Hebrews did exist. The indigenous people of Kamit referred to them as Hekau Khasut (Foreign Rulers) whom the Greek called Hyskos.

The facts are however, that Kamit was once upon a time ruled for a number of years by a group of people called the Hyskos. Historical records indicate that the Kamitic people despised the Hyskos so much that people began to nationalize against them and eventually they ousted the foreign rulers. After the Hyskos were expelled from the country, the Kamitic rulers sought to expand their borders and create an empire to discourage foreigners from ever ruling their country again. Artifacts reveal that the Hyskos left the country but it was not in a grand exodus style as depicted in the movies. The Kamitic sages who were known for chronicling every aspect of their life never made any mention of a thousand or more people fleeing their land due to ten mysterious plagues, especially one which killed every first born. Such as event would have made history and been recorded but it wasn't, thus indicating that *Exodus* is just a story.

As I had mentioned earlier, the problem with the whole *Exodus* story is that it is told from the Biblical perspective. No one even entertains the Kamitic perspective, but when we do. We see that the *Exodus* story was most likely a legend created by the Hyskos. Moses was most likely a Hyskos who was educated and trained alongside the Kamitic royalty. When he came of age and witnessed one of his own in a lower class being mistreated making mud bricks to build their community (not the pyramids or temples which were all built by stone). He became upset, killed the individual and fled. When Moses returned, after shedding all of his Kamitic garments and titles, he became a threat to the Kamitic throne since he was educated and treated like a Kamitic royal. So, rather than having Moses impaled or imprisoned, which was the punishment for his actions, the king of that time chose to expel Moses and his people from the country instead.

xxix

This means that Akhenaten was not a Hyskos and he was not Moses. Akhenaten was the son of the Kamitic ruler Amunhetep III and his name before his conversion was Amunhetep IV. Akhenaten was the husband of the Lady Nefertiti, who marriage was mostly used to cement a treaty between two different cultures. Although many believe that Akhenaten created a monotheistic religion, an analysis of the *Great Hymn to Amun* and the *Great Hymn to Aten* reveals that the Aten religion was actually inspired by the former.

Hymn to Amun Ra

"You (Amun) are the sole one, who made all that exists...He who made pastures for the cattle and fruit trees for men. He who made food for fish in the river and the birds that live in the sky..."

Hymn to Aten

...sole god (Aten) beside whom there is none. You who made the earth as you wished, you alone, All the people, herds and flocks; All upon the earth that walk on legs, All on high that fly on wings..."

In fact, Atenism was not that much different from the already established Amun Ra spiritual system. This is why modern scholars are beginning to describe the Kamitic religion as not being monotheistic or polytheistic but more like henotheistic, which is the belief and worship of a single God, while accepting the existence of other deities. In other words, depending upon the situation is what determines which deity is honored and venerated.

Assuming this is the case would suggest that Akhenaten was most likely a hopeful idealist that was trying to regain control of a governmental system that threatened the king's authority. During Akhenaten's reign, he eliminated priestly bureaucracy and canvased the country with stelas of him and his family basking under the grace of the sun – disc Aten. He dispatched those loyal to him to destroy reference to Amun, in order to establish Aten as the primal godhead. Temples dedicated to Amun were closed and suddenly the largest priesthood in Kamit was out of a job. Akhenaten it seems didn't consider that the Amun's priesthood employed most of the nation. The priesthood, tasked scribes, artisans and many of the people throughout the society in service of the community, while Akhenaten's Aten only employed a few individuals that created stelas of him and his family. Meanwhile, as Akhenaten was focused on the revolutionizing his people spiritual needs, a foreign threat had begun to appear on the country's horizon.

Akhenaten didn't become the heretic king because the Kamitic people didn't respect his spiritual perspective. He went down in history as the heretic king because he nearly bankrupted and destroyed the country; his views created civil discord amongst the people and almost led to Kamit being conquered by the growing Hittite Empire.

Akhenaten exposed in his quest the problem with organized religion. The main pro of organized religion is that it encourages camaraderie and fellowship, but the cons are that fellowship only occurs amongst those with exact external similarities and spiritual development is loss in favor of belief. This is the reason, all of the most horrendous atrocities that have occurred on this planet, were perpetrated by god fearing and believing people. The genocidal treatment of a particular group of people, the enslavement of a people, the bombing of temples, churches and mosques, all the terrorist attacks, etc. were perpetrated and condoned by god fearing Jews, Christians and Muslims.

How could these people who claim to believe in God commit such horrible crimes against humanity? The answer lies in the fact that they all have one common origin. Jewish, Christian and Islamic beliefs all stem from the Hyskos, who were Semitic followers of Set, the lord of chaos, confusion and war. This is not to say that the people were evil, but Set we will see in the future focuses on superficialities (like dogma) – the very things that divides people.

Why Kamitic Shamanism?

It was this conclusion that made me realize that I had been on African trail for some time now because African or African American mysticism is not expressed in the church. As a result, most churches have deteriorated spiritually and focus only on venerating a Supreme Deity, instead of self – mastery and self – development or personal salvation. This is the reason most church officials are not trusted, and why many people are now claiming to be "spiritual" instead of "religious". Churches nowadays have become institutional pep rallies that focus primarily on entertaining the vast majority. Instead of teaching people how to improve their own lives as was done in the past, saving souls has become such big business, that they even have reality television shows dedicated to it.

This is the main reason people from various cultural groups are leaving churches in search of their true spiritual heritage. Many Jewish people for instance are returning to the Kabalistic tradition, Christians are retreating to the Gnostic Christianity and even Muslims are exploring Sufi Islam, while others are taking a more unorthodox route by exploring the Kamitic path. The problem however is that some people with the "savior" mindset have turned the Kamitic tradition into a Kamitic religion by instead of worshipping Jesus Christ, they are now worshipping Osiris. Thereby creating another dogmatic system that divides people based again on superficialities. Fortunately, before a religion becomes a religion, it is shamanism.

Although the word shamanism is from the Tungusic word "saman" and has been used by anthropologists, historians, scientists and laymen alike to describe healers, witch doctors, mediums, priests/priestesses, spiritual healers, etc. According to Michael Harner of the bestselling book *The Way of the Shaman*, a shaman is "a man or woman who enters an altered state at will, to contact and utilize an ordinarily hidden reality in order to acquire knowledge, power and to help other persons." Shamanism is therefore a generic term meant to define individuals all over the world that enter into an altered state to acquire knowledge, power to help themselves and their people.

Based upon archeological research and the fact that shamanic artifacts have been found all over the globe. Anthropologists theorize that shamanism as a system is human beings oldest spiritual system and that it probably first developed as a magical practice used to increase the chances of a successful hunt. Over time it evolved into a full blown system to address the various needs of its people, thus a shaman can be a preacher, spiritual healer, psychic, prophet, magician, etc. but it doesn't necessarily mean that preacher, spiritual healer, psychic, prophet, magician, etc. are a shaman. The key difference as Harner has stated is that shamans have one objective and that is to "enters an altered state at will, to contact and utilize an ordinarily hidden reality in order to acquire knowledge, power and to help other persons."

Therefore, shamanism is the precursor to organized religion. In fact all religions have to some degree an element of shamanism within it but, as soon shamanistic traditions began to systemize their spiritual practices. This is when shamanism ceases being a shamanic tradition and evolves into a religion, which is a set of dogmatic rules and regulations. Once a spiritual tradition declines into a religion, it basically becomes a set of dogmatic rules and mainly a tool of mass control because the individual that controls the spiritual information or theology is able to control the people. This is why religion, instead of bringing people together, further divides them based upon external and superficial differences. Later, the spiritual practices as a result, deteriorate and become empty, useless and meaningless rites done out of tradition with no profound or spiritual connection. This was the case with Akhenaten's Aten religion and the problem all religions have.

Kamitic Shamanism is therefore pro – spiritual and anti – religious, meaning it's not an attempt to tie or unite the Kamitic beliefs and practices with Native American or any other indigenous group's beliefs and practices. The true aim of Kamitic shamanism is to focus upon the spiritual technology or the core concepts and principles of pre – dynastic times and implement them into our life. In Kamitic shamanism, it doesn't matter if you have a religion or not, or if you have a Kamitic image of a divinity because it concerns itself with spiritual concepts and principles, and not the physical and visible forms. For instance, the Yoruba orisha Shango is seen as a later incarnation of the Kamitic Hru. The key to making this type of syncretism is not based upon the intellect but the relationship one has with the ancestral spirits. Therefore, Kamitic Shamanism focuses on establishing and maintaining balance or Maa, and this is how I healed myself.

Finding My "La Manera", My Way, My Maa - Kamta

I was healed because I applied the never changing concepts and principles to my life. I am a happier and more peaceful person overall because I discovered my *la manera* or my w*ay,* which I now understood that the Kamitic people called *Maa.*

Although some people refer to the Kamitic philosophy as Maat, Ma'at or Maat philosophy, Laws of Maat or even Maat Magic, technically speaking I found that Maat is the personification of the first thing the Almighty created to stand upon called Maa. Maa literally means the (Divine) balance, holistic, order, righteousness, justice, truth, or law. Meaning the first thing the Divine created was Truth to stand upon and become the Way. This indicates that Maa is beyond ethics and morals. Maa is similar in many ways to the Chinese Tao, because like gravity. You do not need to be consciously aware of it, to be affected by it. If it works, that is how you know it is the True.

Maa is ideal order, meaning it is not necessarily written in stone or expressed as rules but it is the way things are supposed to be. Maa is therefore, objective meaning that it exists separate from us regardless of what we believe or think about it, like $1+1 = 2$. But when one begins to contemplate the mysteries of the universe and understand that it is based upon the laws of cause and effects. They began to develop what is best called magical thinking or their personal maa (personal balance, order, truth, holistic or personal magical way of life) based upon their affiliations, backgrounds, personal beliefs, influences, etc. Our personal maa is subjective, which means that it exists in our own head like personal memories, emotional experiences, etc. If someone for instance, was frightened by a dog when they were a child and never recovered from this traumatic experience, and as an adult they believe that all dogs are ferocious beast. This is a truth based upon that individual's personal experience, but it doesn't mean that it is the truth for everyone in the world. It is only truth for that individual because they believe in it. Therefore, there is only one Maa (Way) and it is the Universal Truth, but there are several maa (ways) and it is our individual truth (beliefs and thinking). The objective of course is to align our maa (personal truths) with the Maa (Universal or Divine Truth), which governs everything.

Now, an individual's maa (truth) is also his or her personal way of working their mind – spirit. Bluntly put it is "what works for them," in helping them to accomplish their goals in life, because it is based upon their beliefs and thinking. For instance, for some people, laying all of their concerns in the lap of some deity, works for them in getting their goals accomplished, because they believe in the existence of a benevolent supreme deity that cares for them enough to grant their wishes. While for others they may prefer to use visualization combined with affirmations to achieve their goals. As to which method is right or correct, it is the technique that produces the most effective physical results. That is, the wrong one of course is the method or technique, that doesn't work. This is why I call my maa Kamta and it is a Kamitic shamanic tradition that focuses primarily on *obtaining and maintaining Maa through personal spiritual revelation.*

I decided to write a more detailed and lengthy introduction than my previous works to give a better explanation as to how this path evolved, and. To inspire you – the reader – to find your own way, because the time has come for us to stop following dogma and use the power of God within us to issue in the next great era for humanity.

This book has been written specifically for people interested in evolving beyond the fear of dogma to the next level. Since the focus is on mastering concepts and principles. There is no need to mimic what the Kamitic people did or wore thousands of years ago. There is no need for props or other theatrics. You do not need any special attire or any of these theatrics because one of the beauties of shamanism is that it all occurs within the mind. All that is required is that one try to master the concepts and principles, and try to discover your own maa for yourself.

I would like to thank you for your support, and congratulate you on taking steps to create your new life.

Derric "Rau Khu" Moore 6.2014

How to Use This Book

This book like all within this series is an attempt to get people to recognize that African American traditions are a healing art. In order to do this, this book has been designed to be a guide in order to assist you in the process of learning about your superconscious. Following each chapter are lessons that you can use to help you master the material. Of course, it is recommended that before proceeding with the lesson that you read the material in the chapter a few times to get the gist of it.

Chapter 1: Understanding God's Greatest Creation

God's greatest creation is the human mind because after God created the universe and all of the living things within it. God created the human being, who is an exact replica of the Universe on a minute scale. Human beings are therefore a microcosm of a greater Macrocosm, which means everything that exists in the Universe can be found in miniature form within the human being because according to Genesis 1:26, we were made in the image of the Divine. In other words, every human being is genius regardless of our race, ethnicity, culture, affiliations, backgrounds, beliefs, size, shape, etc. We are all expressions of the Divine, thus the divine potential to create exists within us all and it resides within our mind, so what's stopping most of us? What stopping you from reaching your greatest potential? What stopping you from being happy, healthy, rich, successful, etc.?

The answer is that most of us simply don't have knowledge of self. We know our names, our parents, what we like and don't like, but we don't know our true self. We don't know what it means to be made in the image of God, so let's explore this subject a bit more.

Made in the Image of God

Most theologians have shied away from this subject because they are afraid of asking the real tough questions which are "What and who is God?" and finally "who and what is man and woman?"

Fortunately, the wise men and women of Kamit weren't afraid of the answers they would receive. For instance, they knew that the universe consisted of a visible, physical realm and an invisible, spiritual realm which were governed, controlled or willed by one, intelligence, so they sought to find the resemblance within Man and Woman. They discovered thousands of years ago, which was later confirmed by contemporary science in the last 20th century, that the human brain was composed of several parts that interconnect with one another called that reptilian complex, limbic or mammalian system and neocortex.

- The Reptilian brain or R-Complex (Old Brain) also called the lizard brain is the oldest part of the human brain, and is the brain that is most dominant in reptiles. The R-complex consists of the lower parts of the brain known as the brain stem and cerebellum. Scientists believe that this part of our brain developed a couple hundred million years ago and is solely responsible for controlling all of our basic functions such as breathing, circulation, digestion and reproduction. It is also responsible for our body movement and the execution of the "fight or flight" response. Since the R-complex is primarily concerned with our physical survival, all of our behaviors associated with it correspond to the survival instincts of animals like social dominance, territorial and reproduction. The R-complex therefore provides us with the feelings of aggression, anger and lust, which can be seen in territorial fights, displays of anger and lustful mating bouts, which are all automatic or habitual behavioral responses existing in all human beings that are very difficult to alter.

- The Limbic or Mammalian brain (Midbrain) is the second oldest part of the human brain hence and it rests on top of the R-complex. Scientists believe it evolved about a million years ago and consists of the amygdala and hippocampus, which are both necessary for associating events with our emotions and converting information into long tern memories. The mammalian brain therefore links emotions with behavior thereby inhibiting the automatic or habitual response R-Complex.

The mammalian brain is also responsible for all of our primal activities that require us to express our emotions and feelings, particularly anything that has to do with our sense of smell and the need to bond. The mammalian brain is what makes human beings in addition to expressing anger, aggression and lustful, also loving, loyal and protective of one another.

- The Neocortex (New Brain) is the youngest and newest part of the brain. Scientists believe this part of our brain evolved some hundred thousand years ago. It rests on top of the mammalian brain and constitutes five – sixths of the human brain. The neocortex is unique in the sense that it contains two regions – one part to process information and a second, to govern voluntary movement. It is the outer portion of our brain and is responsible for making language (speech and writing) as well logical or rational thinking – possible, thus allowing us to see ahead and plan for the future. Through this brain human beings are able to express themselves using poetry, mathematics, music, etc. because this part of the brain is responsible for development of human language and symbols.

Without becoming a master on the subject, think of it this way. The Reptilian brain is the brain of dinosaurs, alligators and snakes. The Mammalian brain is the brain of dogs, while the Neocortex is the part of the brain that both apes and human possess. This indicates that the two older brains are

3

highly emotional, while the youngest of the three knows no fear, anxiety, etc. It is totally intuitive and inspirational, hence the higher brain functions.

So from a physiological perspective, what motivates us to reach for the double cheeseburger with the buttered grilled bun and fries, instead of sticking to our diet is our reptilian brain or mammalian brain. These two parts of our brain are emotionally dictating what we should do, based upon old memories. This is the reason, before we commit to anything; it is always preceded by an emotionally charged memory.

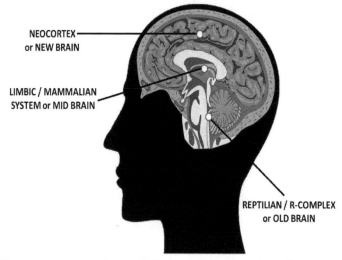

The neocortex doesn't have the emotional power that the older two brain parts possess, but its advantage over them is that has the ability to create languages. This ability to create language allows the neocortex to tap into the older brains and control them through inspiration. In other words, all the neocortex has to do is create an inspirational idea, inspirational thought, etc. and this will motivate the two lower brains to strive for a higher purpose. Therefore, when human beings use symbols they can overcome the reptilian brain and as well as use the mammalian brain for a higher purpose.

Contrary to what some believe, the Kamitic people didn't portray the human beings with animals because they were "aliens." They illustrated these entities on their temple walls with animal and human features in order to convey this mystical, spiritual and scientific truth. For instance, Sabk (Sebek, Sobetk illustrated as a man wearing the crocodile mask) was used to describe men and women that were demonstrating their cold, calculated, sly or reptilian nature.

Hru (Hrw, Heru or Horus in Greek illustrated as a man wearing the mask of a hawk) was used to symbolize the man or woman who relied on the higher functions of the mammalian brain. This was his or her consciousness or what they could see and comprehend, similar to how hawks are able to spot their prey from great distances while in flight and swoop down to capture their target usually around dawn and dusk or nocturnally in urban dwellings (Please note the correlation with the sun).

Osar (Asar, Ausar or Osiris in Greek illustrated as a man wearing white crown) is the most revered because he symbolizes the man and woman that uses his or her higher brain functions – the inspirational and intuitive parts of the brain. In the Kamitic legend, this is the meaning behind Osar replacing Npu (the jackal masked

5

whom we will meet in the future) becoming the new lord of the Underworld.

The Difference between Humans & Animals

We see then that the difference between animals and human beings from a scientific perspective is that human beings have the mental ability to control his or her emotions; while animals on the other hand are ruled totally by their emotions. Man and woman's ability to control their emotions is what allows them to access their higher level of consciousness. It should now be clear why all indigenous and traditional spiritual systems stressed the importance of mental discipline and self – control. The ability to control one's emotions is what allows human beings to access higher levels of consciousness and perceive a reality beyond their physical means. In other words, express themselves as a god or goddess.

A lot of people are afraid of this spiritual truth, which we have just confirmed using science because of limiting and dogmatic beliefs. Their reptilian and mammalian brains have them held hostage, which is why most of the greatest inventions were created by spiritual (not religious) minded individuals. That is individuals who believed in some sort of higher power and understood that it was through mental discipline they could access it. These are the individuals that take humanity to new heights.

Proof that every human being possesses a higher intelligence over animals can be seen in how they deal with death. Although most animals show a sign of intelligence by expressing some sort of remorse when another from its species dies, human beings are the only species with the mental capabilities that goes through elaborate means of caring for the body of the deceased and wishing the deceased peace in a realm beyond their earthly existence. This as you can see requires not only logic and reasoning but an active imagination to be able to perceive such a concept. However, as I am sure you are all aware of, not every human being on the planet expresses his or her higher intelligence. There are some human beings among us that continue to wallow around in the lower places of society with their reptilian brains. Then there are others that refuse to give up the beastly ways of their mammalian brain. This means that our world is dominated by people who are controlled by their animal instincts, yet are trying to develop their higher godlike functions.

Esoterically speaking it can be said that every human being is therefore a soul that has reincarnated from a lower intelligence to a higher one. We don't reincarnate into a bug, dog or bird. No. Consciousness is about evolution, which comes from expansion and growth. This means we can't go backwards, only forward, so our souls were once upon a time bugs, dogs, birds, etc. and we have reincarnated into this human form. This means the reason we find some people acting like beast is because consciously that is where they are, and their purpose in life is to evolve or spiritually develop to the next level.

If this concept is a little confusing, think of reincarnation as grade school. Once a child has mastered the required skills, they advance to the next level of their education. They can't go back and unlearn what they have mastered already. They have to proceed forward and this forward movement is the expansion of their consciousness. However, there are some students that are a little slow in mastering the required skills and they have to be held back.

7

Once they mastered the lesson, they too are allowed to advance forward.

It was this understanding that led the ancient sages to realize that human consciousness was a very complex subject. We are all at different levels of awareness because we have all had different experiences; therefore we have all mastered a different set of skills. From a superficial perspective it would appear that we are all different but we are all striving for the same thing, a higher consciousness.

So to express this theory and assist one another in development, the Kamitic sages divided the mind – spirit into nine spiritual divisions (incorrectly called the nine souls by archeologists). For simplicity purpose these nine divisions can be subdivided into three parts which we all possess and they are: the ba (superconscious), the sahu (subconscious) and the ab (conscious).

The Ba: The Superconscious & Intuitive Part of Our Being

In many spiritual traditions the superconscious realm is commonly called the Heavens, the Upper World, and the Pure Land. In the Kamitic tradition it became synonymous with the southern region of Kamit called Upper Kamit, KAMTA or the Black Lands signifying that it was abundant, mysterious, rich and fertile. It therefore is all knowing because all experiences are simultaneous and omnipresent. It contains the memories of all living beings throughout time. For this reason Swiss psychiatrist Carl Jung called it the collective unconscious because, it is the collective consciousness of all living beings, and. It is the part of our mind that connects us with the living power of the universe.

8

The ba (superconscious) has no fears, and no restrictions because is the higher self or the divine spark that contains the Divine's Eye, which sees the interconnection and shared completeness of everything that exists. Its specific position in the body is the neocortex of the brain and the heart. This is the reason whenever we are inspired by the ba we feel loved, wise, complete, whole, creative, free and peaceful. At the same time the ba also inspires others, which means the ba is a multitasked on a universal scale.

The ba is the most intuitive and most creative part of our being, because it is omnipotent, omniscient and omnipresent. It is pure creative and intuitive energy, and the source of all major breakthroughs, hunches, flashes of insight, inspiration, motivation and new ideas. It is responsible for bringing us bright ideas outside of our learning experience and helps us to see things in a brand new way. Whenever a new idea, new innovative product comes out, it is usually the ba that was the driving force behind it, because the market was saturated with old ideas. Although the ba inspires a lot of positive emotions, the main emotion associated with it is *Love*. This is the reason all of the great sages, martyrs, saints, etc. in every myth, legend, tradition, and religion focused upon unity, peace and happiness through Love.

The Sahu – The Subconscious & Habitual Part of Our Being

When indigenous people say that everything is conscious like birds, other animals and inanimate objects like plants, stones, crystals, cars, plastic, etc., they were referring to the fact that all living beings have a, physical body awareness called the sahu. The sahu is the extremely logical and

9

habitual part of all physical beings that governs the physical and autonomous body functions such as, the assimilation of cells, digestion of food, the transporting of oxygen through our blood stream and so on. Simply put, it controls all of our bodily functions that occur without our conscious thought or input. Everything that occurs within our body automatically is controlled by our sahu. Our sahu like our ba is a multitasked but on a personal level.

Everything that physically exists owes its life to its sahu because the sahu is the awareness that governs all physical things. The sahu is also responsible for physical evolution and therefore contains the surviving memories of everything that once lived including genetic memories. For instance, ever notice how insects seem to become immune to bug sprays. From a shamanic perspective it is because the sahu of the insect adapted, thereby developing a tolerance and immunity against the spray. In other words, it can be said the sahu of the insect remembered what occurred in the last life.

The sahu is the source of all of our emotions and is responsible for storing all of our personal beliefs, emotions, learned skills, personal memories, past experiences, as well as our good and bad habits. This is the part of the mind that we have learned to depend upon the most because in our early stages of development, it helped us to physically survive. For instance, we know not to place our hand over fire for too long because our sahu reminds us that if we do so for too long, the fire will burn. So, our sahu is responsible for storing everything we believe and remember in our muscles, and it associates all of our memories with our emotions. Hence, bad thoughts are triggered by painful memories, which in turn yield negative actions and behaviors. Good thoughts are triggered by pleasant memories, which in turn yield positive actions and behaviors. Since the sahu directly

10

corresponds to our physical experience, many have incorrectly referred to it as our soul, but in truth it is our physical body awareness or lower Self and it corresponds specifically to R-complex and brain stem. This is the reason when we are put into a position where we must change. We feel separate, defensive, fearful, doubtful, worrisome, etc.

The sahu (subconscious) is great when it does what it was designed to do, but problems arise in our life because our sahu cannot make decisions and it associates everything that we learned according to our feelings. This means good memories are associated with good feelings and bad memories with bad feelings. Sounds great at first but if you like candy, desserts and fatty foods, your sahu will associate these foods with good feelings. Obviously we know that we can't physically survive by eating junk food, but this is not how the sahu thinks. If it were left up to the sahu, it would convince us to only eat the foods that we like versus the foods that we need for our body to get the proper nourishment, because it is like a child. Just like children, the sahu only encourages us to do what we like, because it detests change thus making it a home for all of our negative emotions.

Tired of your life going in the direction it is going and you want to change it, but find it hard to do. It is because the child in you, the sahu doesn't want you to change. It doesn't like learning anything new. The sahu doesn't like change so it will make every excuse it can to keep you from learning that new subject. Anytime and every time we try to try to do something different, it is the nagging, complaining, spoiled brat part of our spirit that fights your wishes, all because it likes things the way they are and doesn't want to change. If we allow our sahu (the subconscious or the child) to dictate how we should live based solely upon what we like and don't like, instead of what we need and don't need. It will create

11

two psychological maladies: pscyhosclerosis and a type of homeostasis.

- Psychosclerosis is the hardening of the mind – spirit, where one becomes so rigid, inflexible and dogmatic in their thinking. That they will not allow any kind of change to occur in their lives, thus leading to a feeling of lack of love and enjoyment, as well physiological complications such as immune deficiencies, cardiovascular illness and other health problems.

- Homeostasis is the unwillingness to change because of past events. As a result, we psychologically are stuck in the past because we fear change.

This is why in many spiritual traditions. The sahu realm is commonly referred to in myth as the Underworld, Hades, Hell and the Lower Kingdom believed to be full of monstrous beings that test one's character. All of the great stories and myths about dragons, demons and other monstrous beings that frighten us are about overcoming our sahu, which corresponds to the reptilian brain and brain stem.

In the Kamitic spiritual system, the sahu became synonymous with Lower Kamit – or TASETT the Red Lands because of the host of obstacles one had to endure while traveling through the desert lands. TASETT is fallow ground, which is why it represents the classic hero journey one has to undergo in order to reclaim one's divine birthright. Although, not all of the emotions governed by the sahu are negative, the main emotion or motivational force that the sahu is known for is *Fear*. Therefore, the central theme in dealing with the sahu is always the same. You can't get to heaven, the prize, your divine inheritance, the Upper World, KAMTA, etc. until you face and conquer your *Fears*.

The Ab – the Spiritual Heart, Human Conscious or Human Soul

The ab is the conscious part of our being that the Kamitic sages described as our spiritual heart or soul. It is the "I Am" part of our being that neurologists have found is focused in the center of the brain and is associated with the mammalian brain, as well as the heart. The ab – soul is what makes us relational, so that every time we see something outside of our physical body experience. In order to identify with it we associate with it by saying, "I." For instance, "I am a man (woman). I am from town. I am 23 years old. I am…" Through our ab we have the right to be whatever it is that we choose to be, but in the process of identifying with everything outside of our being. We get lost and are forced to ask ourselves "Who Am I?" because "I Am this" or "I Am that" whenever I choose to be.

Unlike the ba, which is multitasked on a universal level and its' opposite the sahu, which is multitasked on personal level. The ab is what can best be described as single-tasked meaning it works best when it focuses on one thing at a time. In our busy fast paced world, we often praise people who are multitasked, but it has been discovered that it is singletaskers that are actually more successful because they actually follow through thoroughly in completing a given task. As compared to a mutitasker whose attention is scattered and focused on answering texts, responding to emails, while driving a car, trying to grab something to eat and not miss an appointment, etc.

The whole idea of relaxing, developing single mindedness, increasing awareness, avoiding distractions, improving memory or anything that deals with improving self are all forms of meditation based upon the true functioning of our ab to focus on one thing at a time. This is why we are encouraged to do something simple like take a walk, watch the sunrise or sunset, listen to one song (or chant) numerous times, watch one bird or the details of some other animal like the movement of ants. Other activities like raking the leaves, cleaning the house, etc. are all tasks that forces us to focus on the details and specifically place ourselves in the moment.

In fact in various spiritual texts and disciplines we find arguments supporting single tasking versus multi-tasking. For instance, it is said that when Zen master Shunryu Suzuki was asked how he teaches his students about consciousness, he replied "I just try to teach my students how to hear the birds sing."[1] We find mention of singletasking even in the bible, for instance in Luke 10:38 – 42, Jesus was teaching his disciples in Mary and Martha's home when, Martha interrupted him. Noticing her distress, Jesus said to Martha, "My dear Martha, you are worried and upset over all these details! There is only one thing worth being concerned about. Mary has discovered it, and it will not be taken away from her." In this story Mary symbolizes an individual that focuses on what is most important at that time, while Martha symbolizes the busy and often worried mind of a multitasked individual.

Simply put, the ab is what gives us "common sense". When we have common sense we have a holistic view of life because our ab is fully aware. We understand the cause and effects; we see the importance of certain things and have taken the necessary responsibility, hence it is common sense. For example, why do we need to make laws and have law enforcement, police and fine people for texting and driving? It

[1] Chadwick, David and Suzuki, Shunryu *To Shine One Corner of the World: Moments with Shunryu Suzuki.* Broadway; 2001

14

should be obvious of the dangers, but for many it is not because they lack common sense or lack awareness. The reason they lack awareness is because their ab is multitasking. When it is understood that this is not our ab's purpose, through practice we can improve our life by simply focusing on one thing at a time.

The Divine Perspective and Human Perspective

The ab – soul therefore gives us the ability to express our individuality through free will and choice. Since it basically has no memory, but gives us the ability to make choices and decisions. The ab shapes our daily lives based upon the attitudes and ideas that we identify with and the events and people whom we associate. In other words, our ab (conscious) gives us the right to either identify with the *Love* from our ba (superconscious) or the *Fear* from our sahu (subconscious). If we choose to identify with the Love from our ba, we acquire a ba – perspective that makes us optimistic, wholesome, faithful, purposeful, wise, loving, lucky, harmonious and peaceful. If however, we choose to identify with the Fear from our sahu, we obtain a sahu – perspective that makes us anxious, fearful, worrisome, angry, pessimistic, ignorant, unlucky, doubtful, and quarrelsome, etc. This is important to understand because the perspective we choose to follow also determines how events occur in other areas of our life.

For instance, if you have ever tried to advance in your chosen career, improve your relationships, increase your finances, etc. and found it difficult (if not impossible) to complete. It is usually because these three parts of our being (ba superconscious, ab – soul/conscious and sahu – subconscious) are not completely unified. To understand how these three divisions of our being work, imagine there is a fruit tree and it represents life.

The invisible creates the visible.

Now, if we don't like the fruit that the tree is producing, because they don't taste good, they are too small or it is not enough of them. How do we go about changing them?

What most people would do is place emphasis on the fruit, but what we have to remember is that it is not the fruit that creates the tree. It is the seed and the roots that create the fruits. What this means is that it is what lies underground that creates what exists above ground. In other words, it is what we don't see that creates everything that we see. So if we want to change the size, taste, the quantity, etc. of our fruit, we need to place our attention on the seed and the roots. Thus, *it is the invisible that creates the visible*.

Because human beings are a part of nature and not above it, we are just like the fruit tree, which means in order to change our fruit. We have to go to the seed and the root of our being. Therefore, the trunk and fruit of our being is the sahu. The seed and roots of our being is our ba. Since we all have a ba, which means we all have the divine ability to create solutions and solve problems perfectly.

The obvious question that comes to mind is why don't we do it? Why do so many people have so many problems in their lives and it seems to be escalating? The short answer is because most of us don't have a paradigm that encourages this type of thinking. Does that make sense?

Well, let me explain it this way. We all have had great ideas pop into our heads. Instead of us doing something one way, the idea pops into our awareness to try it another way. Most of us when we get these bright ideas agree that it would work and solve a lot of problems, but most of us don't follow through because we have a contradictory thought that visits us. We talk ourselves out of following through with this bright idea because we don't trust this inner genius that dwells within us. The reason we don't trust this inner genius – our ba – is because for many of us when we were children. We were discouraged from being creative and told not to trust our intuitive self in a number of ways but only trust that which we can access with our five physical senses. For instance, as children many of us were told not to daydream because it is a waste of time. Another way children are strongly discouraged which often goes unnoticed, is that unless we have exceptionally great artistic or musical skills. We are told that artists don't make a lot of money. As a result, whenever a new idea comes into our awareness, it has to literally fight in order for it to become a physical reality. This is the same reason; many of us have problems because when it comes to sticking to our diets, managing our behavior, improving our finances, etc. It is all due to the fact that we don't trust our ba.

The good news is that our ba doesn't go away. It simply becomes latent until it is needed, which is why in

17

times of emergency we hear of people accomplishing impossible feats or receiving a bright and new idea. The reason this occurs is because new ideas come to us whenever we are decisive and clear.

Sahu
(Subconscious – Lower Self)

Ba
(Superconscous – Higher Self)

Our ba is like a muscle. The more we use our ba, the stronger it becomes. Not only that, because the ba is omnipotent, omniscient and omnipresent, it makes everything that we want based upon what we say and do. In other words, the ba creates serendipitous and synchronicity events, which makes us feel like we were in the right place at the right time for a particular event to occur. This means that whatever we focus our ab – soul on for a continuous amount of time. The ba will create and manifests it in our life physically.

Therefore, any goal, idea, thought, etc. held in our ab – soul will be brought into reality (our lives, our experience, etc. through our ba – the superconscious mind). This includes both positive and negative ideas as well, which is why it is important to keep our ab – soul (or spiritual heart/mind) on what we want and not on what we don't want. If we don't want something to occur we should not think, imagine or visualize it, because it only gives it power. Instead focus or keep in your ab – soul (heart) on the things you hold dear and want to manifest physically.

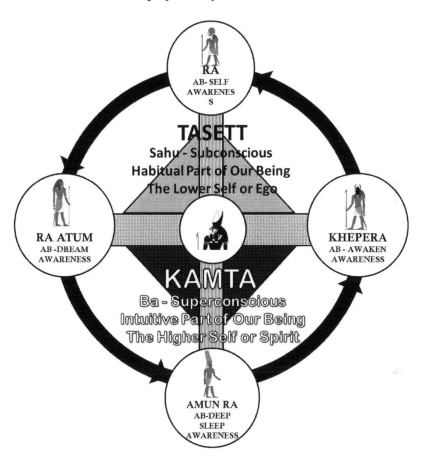

Simply put, whatever is in our ab – soul (good or bad) continuously will manifest itself physically. By continuously, I mean if you entertain that thought in your mind from daybreak to the evening, it will manifest itself physically in your life.

Therefore, we need to give power only to that which we want and the only way to do this is by keeping in mind. That the purpose of the sahu (subconscious) is to help us to physically survive, while the purpose of the ba (superconscious) is to creatively solve any problems that we have to ease living. In other words, since the sahu is habitual and our ba is intuitive. When we constantly remind ourselves what we want by talking about it, affirming it, imagining it, symbolizing it using metaphors, visualizing and finally doing it. We are able to bypass our sahu and sow an idea into our ba, which will provide us with the energy, creativity and wisdom to make our idea a physical reality. So, we just need to bypass our sahu and pass our message (wishes, etc.) on to our ba.

What is Spiritual Development?

From the above we see that we all have three parts of our being that are constantly interacting with each other. These three parts based upon the decisions we make in life determine our temperament and how we interact with others, thus creating our spiritual paths. These paths can be symbolized by the three major crowns of Kamit.

If for instance, we choose to give into the whims of our sahu (subconscious part of our being). We follow the path of the **Red Deshret Crown**, which means generally speaking, we are ignorant, lazy and live in fear. It means we have a poor ability to recall memories and show little consideration or regard for others. Most on this path are brash, coarse, and immoral and are prone to violence. They may be stubborn

20

and inattentive to those around them. They usually show little or no desire to improve physically or mentally, or lack the will power and self–discipline to do so, because they are more concerned with eating, drinking, sleeping or engaging in sexual activity (or sexual perversions). Most go to church, a temple, mosque, etc. totally out of tradition, because they really have little to no interest in spirituality of God. Since individuals on the Deshret path are sensory driven, they easily become depressed or sorrowful. They overeat and consume processed "fast" or "junk" foods regularly. Most can only find pleasure from external sources and many will complain about their positions and relationships with others, because they lack the motivation to take responsibility for their life to change it themselves.

Because those on the Deshret path are slow to move, it usually takes a traumatic or catastrophic event to motivate them to improve their health, donate their time to a particular cause, donate money to a charity, etc.

If we choose to live our life based solely upon our ba, we choose to follow the path of the **White Hedjet Crown**, which means generally speaking, our temperament would become controlling and domineering. The path of the Hedjet crown begins as a peaceful and humbling path, due to some catastrophe or unplanned event, so individuals on this path usually lose their humility. They eventually began to seek and control others. These individuals after having an unexplainable event seek to expand their intellect but usually for the wrong reasons. Consequently, the more knowledge they acquire the more they are able to flaunt and use as a means of control. Since they understand that there is something more to life, many of them look beyond the simple stimulations of food, sex, sleep, etc. and focus more on higher intellectual pursuits.

These individuals have a tendency to bore easily because they are only able to associate with those in their circle. To others they appear to be unapproachable. Simply put, no one wants to go to a party, festival, movie or funeral and hear someone psychoanalyze the entire event.

The good thing about those on Hedjet path is that they are very ambitious, brave, courageous and highly intellectual. Most on this path are usually health conscious, spiritual minded individuals that often abstain from alcohol and tobacco for purely intellectual reasons. (If they do consume alcohol and tobacco, it is easily abused as well as strong coffees and teas.) The drawback for Hedjets is that their positive traits can very easily make them cynical, rude, manipulative, selfish, arrogant, highly critical and sometimes easy to anger individuals with ascetic lifestyles. Most Hedjets are usually intellectually rich but economically and socially poor. What most don't understand is that usually Hedjets had to develop this temperament in order to escape or survive some catastrophe or traumatic event they experienced in the Deshret path.

 If we however, choose to live our life based upon our ab, we choose to follow the path of the **White and Red Pschent Crown**, which means generally speaking, our temperament is a balanced between the two. Those individuals on the Pschent path, like us all, were on the Deshret path but were placed on the Hedjet path by some unplanned event. After spending time on the latter and tired of not being able to interact with others or simply enjoy life. The Pschents evolve and spend a considerable amount of time learning how to balance the best of the Deshret and Hedjet into one.

The Pschents are intelligent, health conscious, calm, content, humble, polite and considerate individuals, with strong wills, that are focused on self – improvement or spiritual pursuits. They are health conscious individuals that can and will occasionally drink a beer because they are not bound by any rules, laws or dogma but moderation.

They respect the beliefs of all individuals regardless of how foolish they may appear because they recognize that they were once fools. They are usually quiet and reserved in their speech because they have learned to watch their actions and words and those of others, which make them excellent strategists. Most Pschents have a strong connection with God and faith in themselves. They do not rely solely upon religious devotion or intellectual understanding, but combine both. This allows them to see the Divine in every religious practice. Pschents can best be said to be the followers of all religions and at time belonging to none, because their only true religion is a clear conscience or peace of mind.

By understanding what path (temperament) you on will help you to understand where you and others stand spiritually. For instance, understanding that someone is on the deshret path would mean that spiritually speaking. This individual is devoted to religiosity, meaning they feel more at ease with an authoritative figure telling them what and what not to do. Discussing spiritual concepts with this individual would simply be a waste of their time and energy because figuratively speaking it is beyond their understanding. A hedjet individual would love to discuss spiritual matters because it is right up his or her alley. Intellectually this is how they would connect to the Divine. A pschent on the other hand would see every experience from working in a soup kitchen to meditating, or making money, etc. as a means of connecting with the divine, because they see no distinction between what is mundane or spiritual.

Spiritual development is therefore about advancing or evolving from the Deshret to the Pschent. We see that we all go from one extreme to the other in order to find balance, which means that the ultimate objective is to rise to the Pschent path.

Lesson 1:
Using Suggestions to Set Goals, Improve Memory & Declare Simple Miracles in Your Life

Goal Setting

Setting goals is a very effective way of getting your ba and sahu to take a more cooperative role in your life. Goals it must be understood are achievable objectives that brings happiness or personal fulfillment when they are not tie to people and things. Since our ba and sahu cannot tell the difference between what is real and imaginary, or what is happening in the future or what has occurred in the past. When you set a goal, it needs to be concrete and new goals have to be set in order to stay fresh, because goals provide our ba and sahu with vision. If an individual doesn't have any goals in life, they will not have any ambition and won't be happy because they have no personal fulfillment. A person with no goals in life, simply coasts along. Therefore, begin by creating goals on what you want such as a certain type of house, to live in a particular neighborhood, have a certain type of car, etc. You can place your goals into the following categorize: spiritual, personal and well–being, material and relationships (of course not in that particular order).

- Spiritual goals would be a better and closer relationship with the Divine, inner peace, peace of mind, or freedom from anxiety, fear, guilt and worry.
- Personal and wellbeing goals would be managing stress, lose excessive fat, get in shape, reducing the intake of sweets and other useless carbohydrates, curbing excessive drinking or breaking a cigarette addiction, etc.

- Material goals would be a better job, house, financial security, a new car, a wardrobe, etc.
- Relationship goals would be a better rapport with your children, your spouse, coworker, a more active role in your community or parent – teacher association, etc.

When you create a goal for your ba and sahu, they should concrete and specific, measurable, and have a definite time period. For instance, saying you want to be rich is too vague, because rich to one person might be $50, 000 while to another it could be more. You have to be specific and say, "I want $2000, by the end of next month." Then let your ba and sahu take care of the details.

Measurable refers to doing whatever you have to do to make your goal achievable. You can't say that you want to be a doctor and you will not apply for medical school, study or do anything to make your goal manifest. At the same time you can't complain that you don't have what you want if you are working to get it.

The purpose of creating a time period for your goal is that prevents you from procrastinating. When you don't set a time limit you will take forever to do one thing. Note that some of your goals might take a bit of time. For instance, if you are just starting college and you want to be a physician, you will have several goals with the main and ultimate goal being your doctorates, so keep this in mind. Don't fret however, because it is the same process.

For instance, I wanted a new bed and furniture before the following month. I wasn't sure how I was going to get it, but I just kept the idea firm in my mind that I wanted it and I was going to get it. I had mentioned it to a few people but I didn't obsess over it. Several weeks had passed by and I got a call from a friend of a friend who was moving and they wanted to get rid of a brand new queen size bed. All I had to do was get it moved into my home. A couple of weeks after, a coworker wanted to buy some new furniture and was willing to give me a couch and love seat for $300. All I had to do was help them move it on to their truck so that they could deliver it to my house.

Another time, I had been, wanting a new television for some time now. So, after several months, I finally decided I was going to buy one. I talked to a mutual acquaintance who worked at an electronic store, to see if they had any sales. She told me she bought one and didn't even use it, but that she would give it to me for free. Once I got it, the remote was lost, but no complaints. I simply expressed my gratitude and stay optimistic. Then someone gave me a universal remote. The purpose of sharing this with you is not to get you to get everything for free but to show how the ba and sahu work.

As I stated earlier, your happiness comes from achieving these things, not from the things itself or people for that matter. This is why it is important to constantly create new goals.

Now, most of us have goals, but where we fail is in creating new goals. This combined with our lack of understanding about our ba and sahu in the past would cause problems later on. So once we get that job, that car, the house, etc. (which are all concrete goals), the anxiety, fear and worry would set in because we begin to wonder how are we going to pay for these things or what happens if this or that happens. Again, the anxiety, fear and worry set in because we didn't understand how our mind works. Fortunately, it is a new day, and we know now that we shouldn't concern ourselves with how the ba and sahu makes things work.

27

When you create goals, it is best to keep them to yourself and not share them with others. Most people will discourage you from achieving your goals because they weren't given the vision you were given, so they can't see where you are going. It is best then to not even share your vision with them, and if so only give a limited amount of details. Also, try to avoid reading magazines, viewing articles, watching television programs and other outlets that would contradict what is in your ab (heart) for your ba and sahu.

Using Affirmations & Declarations

Earl Nightingale wrote in the *Strangest Secret*, "You become what you think about all day long", which means the most important thing we need to do is to learn how to manage our thoughts.

But a lot of us have it wrong. Many of us choose to see before we believe. We want to have a $1000 dollars before we can be happy. We want to be healthy before we can imagine being healthy, and frankly that's not how it works. You can't allow your present situation or emotions to dictate how you should feel. If you do, you will never be happy or achieve any of the things that you want. The same can be said when you complain about your present situation. If you complain about how much money you don't have, how bad things are, etc. You are simply denying yourself of your divine potential by having things dictate your happiness.

You have to change this around. Your driving force for success comes from your thoughts. This means if you want to be healthy, you have to think about what you would do if you were healthy and maintain that thought. If you want to increase your finances you have to think about what you would do if your finances were the way you want them to be

28

and let that motivate you. If you want to be successful, then you have to hold in your mind thoughts of what success means and let that motivate you towards your goals.

When you use your thoughts to guide you towards your goals, you align yourself with your ba – superconscious, which will do what, is necessary to make your dream a physical reality. Once you align yourself with your ba, there is nothing you cannot accomplish.

Now, one of the simplest ways of achieving this is by using our mental – spiritual faculties through repeating positive declarations. Declarations are different from affirmations. When you repeat an affirmation, you are stating something that has not already happened or occurred. A declaration on the other hand is stating something that you have the intention of making true. It is more like a command, whereas an affirmation is more like a wish. Remember, we are all made in the image of the Divine, which means whatever we say with conviction will physically manifest. This is why it is important that we choose our words carefully and refrain from speaking negative about ourselves by saying, "I am no good. I am so stupid. I am dumb. I will never get it. I will never be happy, "and so on, because if you believe that you are stupid. Then you will act stupid and people will perceive you as being stupid because our thoughts (for whatever reason) have the ability to influence others as well.

This is why it is to our advantage to repeat affirmative declarations that invoke strong emotions like, "I love myself. I am sexy. I am great. I am happy. I am successful. I am powerful. I am decisive. I am confident. I earned $4,000 this month. My life is great!" and so on. Your declarations should always be personalized with either "I" or "My" and should either be, "I am, I have, I earned, etc.²" Never use the word "will" or negative connotations like "don't" because this is not a clear instruction to the ba. For instance, if you are quick to anger and you want to break the habit of responding by blowing up. You don't say, "I don't get angry" or "I will not get angry." You would declare or affirm, "I am calm in the midst of a crisis." Instead of saying "I don't eat fatty foods." You would say, "I eat healthy foods for my slim figure." Instead of saying "I am not sick or ill", you would say, "I am in perfect health" or "My body (heart, immune system, mind, etc.) is perfectly healthy."

It is best while repeating this that you imagine what you would do if your desire had already occurred. For instance, I remember when I wanted to heal my legs and be able to walk. I imagined running, playing sports and dancing, while repeating "I am in perfect health. Thank you for perfect health."

The best time to repeat your declarations are before you retire. I have personally found that you should repeat your declaration as many times as you can, anywhere and everywhere. Your declaration is your personal prayer or invocation and it should be repeated as much as possible, until it becomes a physical reality. Remember, the purpose of you doing this is to by-pass your sahu (subconscious) and plant you see into your ba or KAMTA.

An Ancient Method for Improving Memory

---

[2] Those familiar with the 42 Declarations of Maa (incorrectly called the 42 Commandments, the 42 Laws of Maat, the 42 Negative Confessions of Maat, etc.) will now see that these were Ani's personal declarations that he used to program or seed his ba. They were not laws.

As you can see, when you understand the power of the mind, you will find that there are a number of little tricks you can use to help you memorize things as well. For instance, I have personally found that one of the ways to improve our memory since our sahu stores our memories in our muscles based upon emotions, is to repeat what you want to remember while creating a small physical sensation.

To make myself remember a list of items I need to purchase at the grocery store. I tap or poke my finger into my left hand while repeating the list of items I need to purchase. When I am in the grocery store, I ask what is it that I need to get and then I am reminded by my sahu of the list items. I have used this technique to remember other details as well, by tapping my chest or some other body part. Again, it is not about tapping your body part. It is about impressing an idea on to your ba (higher spirit) so that it can remind your lower spirit (sahu) of what you need to remember. I have met some people that can easily recall peoples' names because they associate individual's name with a funny image. I have even heard of people making gurgling or grunting new names because the sensation it makes on the throat muscles leaves a lasting impression. There are many ways you can use this technique. By all means try some out and see which ones work best for you.

Affirming & Declaring with Gestures

Have you ever wondered how certain hand and body gestures got their meaning? For instance, why crossing ones arms at an interview signifies that an individual is either not interested or is angry? It is because hand and body gestures are associated with our thoughts as well. This means that we can also use the above memory technique with declarations. To apply, when making a declaration about simply touch the area of your body that you feel best represents you declaration. Here's a short list of declarations and associated body gestures that can be used, but by all means. If you want to expand upon it or if you find something that works better use it.

My heart is strong and pure	Repeat while placing right hand over your heart
Money comes to me, easily and effortlessly	Repeat with your left hand stretched out and fingers fully extended, then close as if receiving something.
I have brilliant ideas!	Repeat while pointing index finger towards your head.
I am an excellent receiver.	Repeat while outstretching left hand.
I am an excellent giver.	Repeat while making giving gesture with right hand.
I get paid based upon my results.	Repeat while clasping hands together.
I manage my time perfectly.	Repeat with clenched fist up and crossed arms

You can also speak your declarations into inanimate objects because all physical things have a ba and a sahu. This is the reason it is so difficult for some people to manage their money correctly because they think that money is a just a thing. No, money has a spirit, which makes it a type of energy. The form it takes, whether it is a dollar, euro, pesos, yin, jewels, shells, etc. is secondary.

My money works hard for me.	Speaking this declaration over your money will make you a bit more conscientious before spending.
Bless this (water, oil, candle, etc.) to (whatever purpose such as protect, heal, etc.)	This is a general declaration that can be used. Feel free to make adjustments.

Psyching Yourself Up

Have you ever psyched yourself up for a big game, a job interview, or a promotion? We can use this same technique to make ourselves appear to be more intelligent, pretty, successful, stronger, etc. by focusing on a feature of ourselves we want to appear different. Many of us are used to psyching ourselves out by saying, "I can't do it. It's too hard, etc." but as divine beings we are going to turn this around.

To psych yourself up, don't focus on a part of you that you wish was different. Don't even imagine seeing yourself with a particular feature. Simply focus on aspect of you that you admire and praise yourself. For instance, look in the mirror and tell yourself aloud, "Damn! I look good" or "I have a great body!" The idea is that by psyching yourself up with declarations you not only make yourself feel better but you also motivate your ba & sahu to work towards that goal. You don't focus on what you don't like because all this does is motivate you towards that specific area. For instance, if you don't like your tummy fat and you keep repeating and focusing on how to shed the fat around your waist. No matter what you do, it will seem like it takes forever to rid your body of the extra weight around your abdomen. It is sort of like watching a pot of water boil. The more you watch the pot, the longer it seems to take the water to boil. If you focus on your attention on something else, it will seem to occur in no time.

Praise yourself! Talk to yourself! Psych yourself up, but note this only works for small amount of time, meaning that if you aren't making any real commitment to change then you are deluding yourself. Only say you are intelligent if you really believe you are intelligent. Only say aloud that you are gorgeous, handsome, pretty, etc. if you truly believe you are, because you are psyching yourself based upon your inner attributes and qualities, not someone else's physical standards. It is all about attitude. There is nothing wrong with being a little vain about your divinity.

Chapter 2: Exploring the Mysteries of the Superconscious

If you ever tried repeating an affirmation you would notice after some time. A part of you rejects them. A part of you will say when you repeat a health affirmation, "You're lying! Stop lying to me!" The reason is because your sahu is honest and it will only accept what it feels is true.

This is the reason I had to write this book because there is a growing number of people that believe that all they have to do affirm or declare what they want and magically things will fall into place. Affirmations and declarations might work for some things and for some people all the time, but not all the time. This is the reason we really have to work on sowing ideas in the deeper and more powerful superconscious part of our being, because the habitual part will fight us every step of the way.

So, that we are clear. When you are repeating an affirmation and declaration, the thought that comes to you saying that your statement is not true and that you are lying is coming from your sahu, which is basing its statement on your past experiences. What this means is that you have to make whatever you are affirming true. If you are affirming and declaring that you are healthy, then you need to be doing the things that will support perfect health. If you affirm and declare that you are wealthy, then you need to be doing things that wealthy people do such as finding ways to create jobs and other opportunities.

When after repeating your affirmations and declarations, they seem like they are not working. This is because certain events haven't occurred in order for them to physically manifest. This is why your sahu doesn't believe you when you repeat an affirmation, because it doesn't see it. So you have to prove it to the only one that matter – YOURSELF.

Again, if you affirm that you are healthy. Your sahu is really saying, "I don't believe you are. Prove it!" If you affirm that you are successful, your sahu is saying, "Yeah right! Prove it!" Basically your sahu is contradicting (and sabotaging) everything that you affirm and declare because you are dealing with the surface level of your being. In order to quiet the sahu (or at least minimize its chatter). You have to go deeper. .

Understanding the Deeper States of the Mind

Remember our tree example from the last chapter? Remember that our sahu governs the lower level of our being and our ba the higher parts?

Sahu
(Subconscious – Lower Self)

Ba
(Superconscous – Higher Self)

Well our brain is an electromagnetic organ, which researchers have discovered generates as much as 10 watts of electrical power. What this means is that if each one of the nerve cells inside of our brain were hooked up they could power a little light bulb, because like an engine it is able to emanate electrical frequency called brainwaves. The brain has several brainwaves that it is able to function from. The faster the brainwaves the less activity it emanates, while the slower the brainwave the more activity it emanates. The four brain waves are:

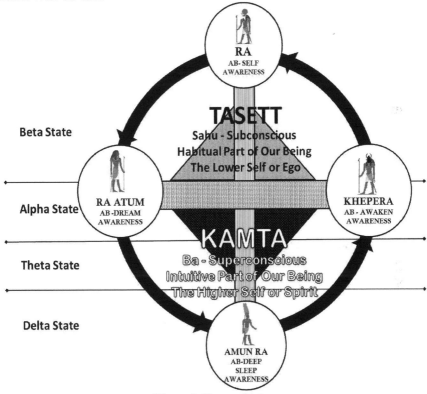

Figure 5: Trance States

- **Beta** – this is the brainwave that we use to function in our daily life. Beta waves range between 15 to 40 cycles per second, indicating that the mind is highly active. When an individual is debating, teaching, speaking, etc. their mind is functioning from this state.

- **Alpha** – is a relaxed state of awareness. Alpha waves range between 9 and 14 cycles per second and the amplitude higher than beta. This is what is commonly referred to as the twilight state.

- **Theta** – is an even more relaxed state of awareness. Theta waves range between 4 and 8 cycles person second and amplitude of the waves are much higher than alpha. If you have ever driven for a long period of time and found yourself daydreaming, but unable to remember the last few miles. It is because the constant repetitious act of long hour driving has become so automatic, that it induced a state of trance. Theta is our dream state or where REM (Rapid Eye Movement) occurs.

- **Delta** – is the slowest and most relaxed state of awareness. Here the brainwave ranges between 1.5 and 4. It never goes to 0 because it would mean that you are brain dead. This is where deep non-REM (Rapid Eye Movement) or dreamless sleep occurs.

So whenever we fall asleep, we move from Beta, to Alpha, to Theta and finally Delta. When we awake from a deep rested sleep we move in the descending order from Delta back to Beta. When we compare these states to the Maa Aankh we see that Beta state we see is above the sahu region, which explains the reason the sahu contradicts our will so much.

Therefore, Alpha state is the most optimal state that we want our brain to function in, in order to sow declarations of change or any idea. If you repeated a declaration and it worked, most likely it was because you repeated it while in

38

the Alpha or deeper state of mind. However, if we go deeper into KAMTA, meaning are brain cycles between 1.5 and 8 – the Theta and Delta state we are able to do much more such as receive insightful dreams and visions, improve our learning skills, and even heal our body, because we are descending closer to our pure state of awareness, the source – Amun Ra.

The ancient knew this which is the reason throughout the world before the birth of organized monotheistic religions. We find that most traditional societies conducted religious performances by chanting, clapping, using rhythmic drumming and flickering light produced by a bonfire, torch or candle, because they were all methods that could put us into an altered trance state. This is the reason to this day; many of these methods like candles are either used separately or in combination with other methods for religious ritual.

The reason this is important to know is because whenever we enter into an Alpha trance state. Our mind – spirit is the most receptive and any message can be sowed into it with little resistance. That's right. Any message can be sown into your mind – spirit by either you or someone else (community, media, society, etc.), which influences your beliefs and actions[3].

The Magic of Alpha State

Here's a little trick that will prove to you how the power of suggestions works. For the longest time, I have been waking up without the use of an alarm clock and you can do it also. While lying in the bed before falling asleep, tell yourself you want to wake up at a specific time. For instance say, "I want

---

[3] It should now be clear why music and movies also put us in trance. In fact, most frenzy is due to media manipulation.

to wake up at 6:00." Then go to sleep without setting your alarm clock and see if it works. Note the time and how close you wake up to the time you desired. Also, note how refreshed you feel upon awakening. If it doesn't work, try it several times more and note your results. The reason this little trick works is because usually whenever we fall asleep we are near the Alpha state. In fact, usually whenever we are physically exhausted. We enter into this meditative state which is the best state to transmit messages into our ba – spirit and use our imagination like the Kamitic ruler Snefru. For those of you who don't know about king Snefru, he was the visionary that came up with the design of a straight edge pyramid.

The way story goes is that before the Great Pyramid was built, the very first massive pyramid that was conceived and constructed about 5,000 years ago the first monumental building in human history was built by the architect Aimhetep (Imhotep) for King Djoser called the Step Pyramid (shown above).

Djoser's descendant Snefru wanted to a pyramid with perfectly straight sides. His monument began as a step-pyramid and was filled in with limestone casing stones. To create smooth sides, but at some point the outer stones collapsed and all that remained was the inner layers. This pyramid is known as the Meidum Pyramid.

Snefru was not pleased with the first pyramid in the beginning so he began creating a second pyramid outside of Darshur known as the Bent Pyramid. This second pyramid started out at an angle of 54 degrees, but cracks in the burial chamber caused the ancient engineers to make adjust the angle to 43 degrees, thus giving it a bent shape. This indicates that Snefru was attempting to make another straight sided pyramid.

Snefru built a third pyramid and this time the whole pyramid was constructed at a 43 degree angle, which is the same angle as the corrected top section. The result was the Red Pyramid. The ingenious idea to build a perfect straight line pyramid was most likely inspired by the solar disc of Ra.

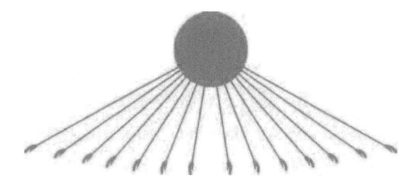

Although, it is not exactly known, but what is known is that Snefru built three pyramids in order to get the sides perfectly straight. This clearly indicates that he was definitely being inspired by his ba and was most likely in Alpha state, which was leading him through the whole trial and error process.

Problem Solving with the Superconscious

If we were to summarize Snefru's efforts they could be that he didn't let his disappointments force him to settle for less. He believed that he was going to construct a perfect straight-side pyramid and he set out to make his vision a physical reality, which became the iconic image of Kamit. This means that when we are faced with disappointments we need to remind ourselves of our goal and believe that everything that happens is moving us closer towards goal. The best way to do this is by focusing on the benefit. The more you focus on the benefit the less time you will have to think about the setbacks.

This is what all successful people do. Athletes don't dwell upon their losses; they focus on winning and all of the fame, endorsements and glory that comes with winning. This is superconscious magic and it is what drives them to train hard. It works because their ba lays out the path for them to achieve that goal.

We need to understand that the purpose of our sahu is help us to learn certain skills and we only acquire them by trial and error, but it is our ba that gives us the inspiration and intuitive wisdom to solve the problems that we face. For instance, imagine a child wanting to be physician. The ba is not going to magically make this child a physician without them going through the proper channels to receive an education. I mean if the child barely learned their multiplication table, there is no way they are going to become a doctor overnight. No, there are certain things that child

43

must learn first and the ba with its omnipotent wisdom is aware of this, so the ba will create a path for us to achieve whatever it is that we want, especially if the goal is a high one. Now, here the thing about this, when the ba lays out this path, it will include in it disappointments, setbacks, obstacles, etc. in order to teach us the lessons we need to achieve our goal.

So, we need to get pass our sahu because not only is limited and based upon our past experiences, but it will fight us every step of the way in achieving our goals with discouraging thoughts and experiences. This is when it pays to understand the nature of the human mind, because knowing this well help you to realize why after hearing the lengthy sermon. As soon as you left the temple, the reason you went back to your heathenish ways because the message was received while you were in the Beta state.

It is important to understand that as a spiritual being inside of a physical body with a soul, we will always have problems in our life, as long as we live. But, we can cope with them by simply learning how to retreat within. When we retreat within the limitations of the sahu are removed so that our ab – soul can obtain a solution from the ba – spirit.

Therefore, whenever we focus or contemplate and begin to daydream, we are in essence engaging in a form of meditation. This may come to a surprise to some because they are under the impression that in order to meditate you need to sit a specific position, and chant a string of unpronounceable words. This is one of the methods for enter into a trance state but it is not the only one. Let's explore some of the other ways of getting pass our sahu, so we can improve our life.

More Methods for Programming the Mind – Spirit

As you have read earlier our sahu (the habitual subconscious part of our being) has been ruling our lives. It is responsible for everything that we have learned and it works great when it does what we want, but when we find ourselves trying to change. Our sahu is the part of our being that puts up the greatest fight. Not only that. If our sahu in any way was traumatized by an event or knows that we don't like a particular thing, because it lacks the ability to make reasonable decisions. It can and will sabotage our conscious efforts because we may have consciously forgotten an experience or forgotten that we didn't want to work so we faked an illness several times, but our subconscious didn't. It interprets everything literally and will actually make the experience a part of our reality. The next thing we know, we are out of a job only because it was raining and we didn't want to go in, or we said something that we really didn't mean to say and it happened. So, in order to limit our sahu's domination over our lives, we need to sow our ideas into our ba, which is wiser and more powerful than our sahu. And, the following are several ways in which this can be accomplished.

Now, most of us have heard that we are only supposed to speak affirmatively, focus on what we want in the present, etc. but usually we don't remember to do this until it is too late because we have no way of reminding ourselves about the how our mind – spirit functions. When we use the Maa Aankh as a guide we can easily remember and discover how to sow new ideas into our mind – spirit. For instance, by following the flow of the arrows and seeing how both the ba and sahu are interdependent upon one another. We see that our mind – spirit is holistic in nature. One of the characteristic of our mind – spirit holistic abilities, is that it

45

is timeless meaning it functions only in the present. The only time we feel and experience sensations in our body is in the present. We don't experience them in the past or the future, but in the present. You might recall an experience that triggers an emotional response, but the experience was stored and based upon a present – day experience. This is the reason the best way to impress an idea upon our mind – spirit is by experiencing it as if it is occurring in the present.

This holistic characteristic also means that our mind – spirit does not differentiate between past, present and the future or what is real versus what is imaginary when used together. In other words, since our sahu is responsible for storing our memories, when not disciplined it will dwell upon past events or worry about the future. When combined with the ba however, time becomes irrelevant, which means when you focus on an idea the ba – sahu views the idea as occurring in the present and registers it as being real. This is the reason for giving yourself positive affirmations and declarations.

If you will recall, holistic is one of the definitions of Maa, which we saw earlier also means truth. This means that our mind – spirit is by nature honest and truthful as well, like that of a child. Notice that before children learn social behaviors they will say whatever comes to mind because they have not learned which action and behaviors are appropriate and inappropriate. Well, the same applies to our mind – spirit. For instance, when classifying something as being "good" or "bad" our mind – spirit lumps everything that is good as being anything that is acceptable and bad and unacceptable by your standards. So if you become angry, upset, disgusted, etc. with someone, our mind – spirit sees it as us being angry, upset, disgusted, etc. with ourselves or something we find to be unacceptable. These ideas then become either empowering or disempowering.

46

In T. Harv Eker's book *The Millionaire Mind*, the author retells how one day while watching Oprah show, the daytime talk show host was interviewing Halle Berry and discussing how she just received $20 million contract, which was the largest contract for a female actress at that time. During the interview the actress stated that she didn't care about the money but fought for the contract in order to blaze a trail for other actresses. Eker recalled that upon hearing this, the first thing he thought and said was, "Yeah right! Do you think I and everyone else watching this show is an idiot?" He claimed that when he realized what he was doing, he immediately tried to neutralize the negative thoughts by screaming at the top of his lungs, "Way to go, girl! You rock! You let'em off cheap!" because he remembered his criticism about Halle may not have affected her, but it definitely was a reflection about how he thought and felt about himself. By resenting her success, he was in essence resenting success for himself.

By congratulating Halle on her success, Eker was identifying to his mind – spirit, that the same successful experience she had, he would like to have as well. In other words, be put in a position where he could say after receiving $20 million, "I don't care about the money. I was doing it for …"

Now when it comes to sowing ideas into the our mind – spirit there is no one proven way that works for everyone, but there are a few things we can keep in mind. For one, the best way to sow new ideas into our mind – spirit is by using our emotions. The more intense our emotions are when associated with an idea, the deeper the impression is made. This is the reason we remember being frightened or attacked by some animal like bit by a dog or snake, or stung by a bee. It is because of the emotion associated with event. The same can be said about the first time we touched something hot or extremely cold. These are all examples of one time learnings because the idea has been deeply sown into our mind – spirit after the initial experience.

Another way of sowing an idea into our mind – spirit is through repetition, which is the way we create habits. Again, if the new idea is accompanied with an emotional experience, then it would take fewer repetitions to impress the idea onto our mind – spirit.

When it comes to changing our beliefs, generally speaking all that is required is that we receive new information, but in order to validate that new information and permanently change our beliefs. We need a new experience associated with this new belief, because if not the old idea which is older will remain. For this reason it is best to examine our old beliefs first and understand why it no longer serves you, before sowing a new belief. In the following chapter we will see how this process is allegorized in the *Story of Osar* where Set symbolizes the old idea, Osar is the new one and Hru is the force attempting to make the idea permanent.

Since our sahu (subconscious) is habitual, lacks the ability to make rational decisions, and associates ideas with our emotions. Symbolic language is another way of sowing ideas into our mind – spirit because they represent ideas and can easily trigger emotions. The most common symbols used are music, symbolic images and metaphors.

Music as a Tool for the Programming the Mind – Spirit

Music naturally is one way of sowing idea into the mind – spirit. Whenever we listen to music it relaxes us and has the ability to put us in a particular mood. When we listen to any particular type of music, while thinking about certain ideas or thoughts, it is associated with each other. This is the reason many people find it easier to study while listening to music. Some people are able to recall what they have studied with ease by simply remember the particular music they were listening to while studying.

Symbolic Images as a Tool for the Programming the Mind – Spirit

Symbolic images are used all the time by our mind – spirit. In fact, this is how our mind – spirit communicates to us in our dreams. The best way to interpret your dreams is not to look at the actual meaning of the symbol but to understand how the symbol in your dream made you feel. For instance, while writing this book a couple of days ago I had a dream where an acquaintance of mine gave me a bunch of his shopping bags while I was standing in line to go to the movies. As I approached the concession stand, I found myself to unable to decide what I want because I was juggling the bags from one arm to the next. In the end, I missed the movie and I woke upset because I interpreted the dream to mean that I was too occupied with my friend's problems to enjoy my own life. So dreams are very important and when you understand the symbolism behind them you can use the same symbols to sow ideas into your mind – spirit.

You can also use symbols as a way of talking directly to the mind – spirit as an archetype, which we will see in the future. Many people who believe in angels, saints, etc. do this all the time. In fact, the one author that made extensive use of this was Napoleon Hill the author of the bestseller Think & Grow Rich. In Hill's book he writes how before he would retire he would imagine meeting the most influential people in his mind's eye like Napoleon Bonaparte, Abraham Lincoln, Henry Ford, Emerson and several others totaling to what he called his Nine Invisible Counselors. Every night he would hold a meeting in his mind with these individuals and ask them to comment on various aspects of his life. With much amazement, Hill stated that even though he knew this was a figment of his imagination, his counselors gave him sound and perfect advice. Hill claimed that during his counseling sessions he would study the lives of these individuals he admire and after several months of meeting with them he noticed that they began to take on individual personalities. So astonished was Hill that he began to meet with others whom he admired including Jesus, Socrates, Plato, Newton Confucius and many others (both alive and dead).

By understanding the nature of our mind – spirit we see that the reason Hill got expert advice from his counselors is because ba used the information from the sahu about these historical individuals as a conduit to respond to Hill's concerns. This is the reason it can be said that the Divine does not care what religion you profess to believe in because truthfully speaking being an Immortal Spirit. God can take on any form.

The purpose of forming your own invisible cabinet of counselors is because as Hill stated, they provide you with various forms of inspiration by giving you practical ideas that you can implement in your life. Many of these individuals that respect because of their greatness can give us plenty of insight on how to improve our lives. For example, understanding that Albert Einstein use to express gratitude to all of the deceased mathematicians and scientists that he respected who came before him, believing that they contributed to his success. Helped me to express my gratitude to others living and dead, thereby making me appreciate and receive more out of life. There are other benefits as well. For instance, by learning that a particular hero or heroine would practice a speech a certain way, take a

nap, study in solitude at midnight, etc. might prove
beneficial to you, because instead of trying to reinvent the
wheel. You can simply follow what someone else has done.
Your counselors can also help you arrive at a decision and
help you solve problems.

The other benefit of having your own counselors is that
the more you read about them and study how they did
things. The more you in an indirect way surround yourself
with their energy. In essence you are surrounding yourself
with great minds, so you are therefore becoming great as well
because you are partaking in their essence, hence the term
archetypes.

Metaphors as a Tool for the Programming the Mind – Spirit

Metaphors can be used to sow ideas into our mind – spirit a
number of ways. Visual metaphors like most cosmograms
such as the Tree of Life, Tree of Knowledge, Medicine Wheel,
Maa Aankh etc. can leave a long lasting impression after
studying them, which results in receiving flashes of insight
that could not be expressed in words.

Verbal metaphors such as stories, tales, legends and
myths are able to reward one with deeper insights as well, as
we will see with the *Story of Osar.*

Tangible metaphors are what are commonly called
miracles or magic by individuals that do not understand the
power of the human mind. All forms of tangible metaphors
act through the unexplainable and unidentifiable laws of
attraction initiated by one's ab – soul (conscious). There are
two principles of tangible metaphors. The first is that "likes
produce likes" (homeopathic magic), which means virtually
any kind of natural phenomenon can be created by simply
acting it out beforehand using natural objects that are in

51

alliance with the individual's purpose. An example of this would be taking a small stone and naming it after a situation or thing you want to rid yourself of, then throwing it over your shoulder into a river. The idea sown into the mind – spirit is not that the stone is being thrown into the river but the situation or thing that it represents because it is believed that whatever happens to the small stone will also happen to the situation or thing the small stone represents.

The second principle of tangible metaphors is that things that have been in contact with each other will continue to maintain contact known as contagious magic. Therefore personal belongings including one's hair, nail pairings, jewelry, clothing, etc. can be used to sow ideas into the mind – spirit. For example, a baseball cap once worn by a famous athlete is believed to continue to radiate the athlete's energy, hence it is considered lucky if worn by a fan and will improve their own athletic skills. Again, it must be kept in mind that it doesn't matter if others don't believe in the efficacy of tangible metaphors, so long as the one using it does.

Symbolic metaphors are expressed in action and gestures. These are usually performed as part of a ceremony or ritual. A ritual is simply a repetitive action done to empower an individual by connecting to the Divine. It takes ordinary objects and combines them with meaningful gestures in order to make something sacred. For instance, think about the Jumping the Broom ceremony where a husband and wife leap over a broom together symbolizing the start of a new life. Then, there's the lighting of the unity candle at wedding where two candles symbolizing two families are brought together to light one candle representing one united family. Again, in order for the rituals to have a lasting effect they have to be associated with our emotions and possibly repeated.

The Superconscious Isn't Magical, but It's the Next Best Thing

Usually when people hear about the magnificent feats of their ba – spirit (superconscious) they or how they are made in the image of the Divine. The first thing they want is magical or miraculous proof, but you have to understand that is not the purpose of the ba. Just because you say you want something doesn't mean that all of a sudden it is going to magically appear out of thin air in front of you. It doesn't work like that. When you hold a particular thought in your ab – heart (conscious mind) affirmatively and visualize it long enough so that the seed is planted deep into your ba. The ba will provide you with a way to achieve your goal.

For instance, if you say, "I want to be rich" it is understood that you aren't already, so you will continue to have this same wish. If however you affirmed, "I am rich" then after repeating this affirmation, one day you will have an idea that will lead you to down the road where you will become rich. This is how the ba works by providing you with solutions on how to achieve goals. It is not a genie. It is your divine spark so respect it and use it accordingly.

The Power of Expectation & Luck

Since the ba creates a physical reality that is consistent with the thoughts and beliefs that we hold in our awareness. If we expect certain events to occur in our life, the ba will create the situation and surround us with the people to make the event occur according to our thoughts and beliefs. This is reason some people it seems are always in the right place at the right time. These people always seem to get the best parking space, when at games of chance, be in the right place to take advantage of an opportunities, etc. It is because these people expect to get what they want and when they don't they don't sulk. They simply move on, accept that someone else needed it, but the next time they still expect to get that parking space, to win that game, etc.

To change your luck, you need to do the same thing. Expect the unexpected from your ba, because if we don't the unexpected will occur. When you don't focus on what you want in life, you will be reminded of the things that you don't want. And, the next thing you know Murphy's Law is in effect. So, focus on what you want and expect what you want to manifest.

Allow the Spirit to Lead

It must be kept firmly in mind that our ba does not function like our sahu. Our sahu as we saw above is extremely logical like a computer. Everything it does has to make sense to it because that is what it has learned. Our ba on the other hand is beyond our intellect because it functions solely on acceptance and faith. What this means is that when working with the ba, everything we do is not going to make logical sense to you or others, because it is based upon a knowing. There are some things you can't always prove to others but you just know. This is the other reason for symbolizing and associating the sahu with TASETT and the ba with KAMTA, to remind us that our sahu and ba are opposites of each other. For instance, we know that in the physical world that the harder we train, work, etc. the stronger the results. Well, when working with the ba, the more physical effort you put into it, the longer it will take for the ba to solve the problem.

Simply said, the ba cannot solve problems if our sahu is worrying and mulling over the issue. The ba cannot be forced or pressured into to completing a task. The ba only

54

creates in a positive and relax atmosphere. Anytime you try to rush your ba to be creative, you will end up messing things up. This is the reason whenever we see someone that is stressed and they are trying to solve a problem. It is only after they relax and take several deep breaths they are able to think and see things clearly.

In order to solve any problem using our ba, all we need to do is create a positive affirmation and visualize it until it becomes a physical reality. This is the only thing we need to do and have faith that our ba will take care of the rest.

We need to relax, have confidence, concentrate on what we want, keep our mind focused and expect that what we want to come to us when we are ready. To remind us not to worry, fret or mull over ideas because it is similar to treating the trunk and fruits of our tree.

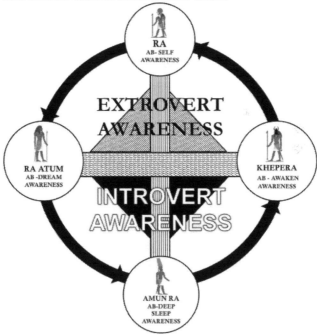

Figure 6: Introverted - Extroverted Maa Aankh

55

TASETT is used to symbolize that our awareness is extrovert and therefore limited. In order to receive a perfect solution from our ba we need to move our awareness into KAMTA or simply introvert our awareness.

When you understand the nature of our mind – spirit we see that the only thing that can prevent us from achieving our greatest potential is our selves – particularly our lower self. To be specific, it is our anxieties, fears, guilt, worries, etc. For this reason to remind us of our greatness we have the *Seven Codes of Maa*.

Seven Codes for Working the Mind - Spirit

The Seven Codes of Maa are not a set of laws and they should not be viewed as being a set of dogmatic rules that tells us what to do and what not to do. They are simply seven principles based upon the Maa that remind us how to utilize our mind – spirit.

1. *"Maa is Truth & Is Based Upon Perspective,"* which means learn to see the drinking gourd as being either half empty or half full.

2. *"Maa is Balance & Is Limited By the Mind,"* means that the only limitations that exist are the ones you set in your mind.

3. *"Maa is Harmony & Becomes What Attention is Focused On,"* means expect something wonderful instead of thinking what might happen.

4. *"Maa is Justice & Doing what is Right, Right Now,* "means stop thinking you are going to get punished or

56

that your life is bad because of some karmic debt. You shape your future based upon the decisions you make right now.

5. "*Maa is Love & Love is Exchange*," means stop working for money (and other material things) to make you happy. True happiness comes from when you share what you do for yourself with others. As, the former mayor Samuel M. Jones of Toledo, Ohio says, "What I want for myself. I want for everybody."

6. "*Maa is Order & Not Coincidence*," means that everything happens for a reason even if you can't understand the cause. Know that every effect is the result of some cause.

7. "*Maa is Propriety & Doing What is Relevant*," which means do whatever works for you because no one knows you except you.

Lesson 2:
Developing Your Intuition Using Symbols & Divination

One of the biggest problems that most of us have is in trusting our intuition. The reason we have problems trusting our intuition is because we live in a society where we hate to be wrong. We all want to be perfectly correct. What we need to understand is that all of this is a learning experience, so if we're wrong. We simply need to learn from the mistake instead deciding never to trust intuition again.

We receive a lot of helpful and insightful information but we fail to act on it because we don't have anyone to validate us. We feel secure only in what our family and friends tell us, because we don't have any faith in ourselves. The reason most of us don't have any faith in ourselves because we have all been in that situation where we took a leap of faith and fell on our face. What we didn't know was that this leap of faith is what is called blind faith.

Blind Faith is where you act if something is true based upon what another has said, even when you don't have any evidence of its validity. There other type of faith is called Understanding Faith, where you have experienced or acquired to some extent, evidence to validate your belief. To give you an example of each, when we were younger and were told to turn on a light switch by our parents. We took their word, because of them being a figure of authority, that when we flipped the switch the lights would come on, which is Blind Faith. After years of changing a light bulb and turning the light switch on ourselves we know that the lights will come on, and this is Understanding Faith. Blind Faith starts us out on our journey, but it is Understanding Faith that carries us along the way.

In order to develop your intuition you have to have Understanding Faith, which comes from observing the various signs and symbols that occur in nature. For instance, if you know that a snake bite is poisonous, when you are around someone and the image of a snake comes to mind. This is your intuition giving you a warning not to trust this individual. But many times we aren't sure if this is true or not, so the following exercise will help you.

Learning to Trust Your Intuition

This is a very simple and effective exercise for developing your intuition. Since one thing about the sahu is that truthfully it cannot lie, it can learn how to lie but typically speaking it does not lie, which is the reason it thinks when you are affirming you are lying. Tell yourself a true statement like your name, age and who your parents are, etc. Notice how when you tell yourself the truth how it makes you feel. Make note where the energy went and how it feels. Was it in your heart, your head, your stomach, etc.? Did it feel light, empowering, etc.?

Now tell yourself a bold face lie like lie about your age, your height, etc. You can say something like "I am 12 feet tall." Once you lie, note how it feels. Did your heart race? Did you breathing become irregular? Note this all.

The reason for doing this is because now you know when your ba is speaking and when your sahu it reacting. When you feel this same energy that you felt when you lied to yourself. Then you know that your sahu is giving you false information based upon your anxiety, fears, guilt, worries, etc. When your ba is speaking you will know because of the emotional signature if leaves behind.

59

You can use this method when faced with a decision and you need to know if you can or should do something. You simply ask a "yes" or "no" question. For example, "Would it be a good idea to go out tonight" If you feel the answer is "Yes" then it should have that same true emotional signature if it is coming from the ba.

This exercise will help you to take a pause in your awareness and make you think before reacting to every situation you are faced with. You will notice that the more you practice this exercise on a daily basis, the sharper your intuition will become.

Having Faith in Your Intuition

It is important to understand that it is quite natural to be skeptical when we receive solutions that come into our awareness, but the only way to gain confidence is to try the solution out. I know this difficult for many because most of us were raised in a Western society where emphasis is placed upon what we see, feel, hear, smell and taste. We always seek the opinions of others instead of trusting our own higher self, but the question we should all ask ourselves is, "How many people have to approve, confirm or validate us in order for us to believe in ourselves?"

We have to understand that some people will believe in us and some people will not because we all have our own opinions. This means we need to stop trying to please other people and please the only person that matters, which is our self. Understand that what is meant by pleasing ourselves is that it must be a truth that works for us. If most people in our society would follow their soul instead of listening to the opinions of others, the world would be a better place, because they wouldn't be so reactionary to everything. The problem is that most people don't trust themselves.

60

So, we have to get to the point where we don't care about the opinions of others and live our lives based upon what works by developing an inner knowing. The more you live truth, the sharper your intuition, the more proactive you become and the more you will find that your ba – spirit is your best ally. Eventually, the more you rely upon your ba and develop a truthful way of living. The more you will begin to understand why it is important that you don't believe anything unless you have tried it out for yourself.

Simple Way to Meditate

One of the side effects to pausing and depending upon your intuition you will notice is that you also temporarily changed your state awareness by meditating. Meditation is just another word for contemplation, which means you have simply suspended your thoughts and focused on one subject at the time. Meditation you see it is not complex, but there are two reasons this has been such a difficult subject to grasp. The first reason is that there are many ways to meditate, but people often led to believe that there is only one way and if you aren't doing it this specific way then you are wrong. This is totally untrue. The second reason a lot of people don't want to meditate is because a lot of spiritual minded individuals have made meditation out to be a chore. I mean think about it. When was the last time you heard someone say with excitement and enthusiasm, "Hey! I am about to go meditate!"

If people understood that meditation is going within to get answers from your higher self or from the Divine. I think they would have a better attitude towards meditation. This is the reason any time I introvert my awareness, meaning I go into an Alpha, Theta or Delta state of awareness. I refer to it as "Going to KAMTA". When I go into KAMTA it is either to get answers or to do some work on my lower spirit – sahu. You are purposefully daydreaming.

The easiest way to go into KAMTA (the spiritual realm) is to go into a quiet room and simply relax your body and let go of all the tension in your muscles. If you are a novice you might want to close your eyes to minimize distractions. Don't think about anything. Just let your mind run free and any thoughts that come to your awareness, simply let them pass through. The more you relax, the more you will notice that your breathing will become deeper and slower. You will know that you have arrived in the Alpha state when you feel pulsing energy, see beams of light, your body feels hot or very cold, or your body feels very rigid. These are all signs that you have passed into the spiritual realm. Note that if you fall asleep it simply means that you went too deep and you are either in Theta or Delta state. You simply have to gauge yourself. It is best if you are a beginner to avoid lying down to avoid falling asleep and trying doing this by sitting down until you get the hang of it. It may also be helpful to slowly count from 100 to 1 mentally.

To come out of this trance state, is like waking up. Simply try to bring awareness back into your body by gradually speeding up your breathing. You can also try rubbing your feet on the floor or rubbing your hands together. Whatever you do, refrain from just getting up. To do so, might cause you to feel a little droopy. When you have brought your awareness fully back to the Beta state, say "Thank you".

Practice going into KAMTA on a daily basis, until you become proficient at enter with no problems. The more you practice this, the more relax you will feel, and you will notice that you will be slower to anger.

Trance Triggers

The purpose of this exercise is to show you how you can program your mind – spirit with the simplest of commands to go into trance. In fact, in many non – Western cultures, they use what could be called mind state triggers to automatically send them into a trance state. Some of these methods are rhythmic sounds created from chanting or clapping, a steady drumbeat, or flickering lights produced by bonfires, candles and torches. To create your own trance trigger, enter into KAMTA and once you are feeling the Alpha state tell yourself the following, "I will automatically enter into a trance state, whenever I (name the trigger you want to use)."

I have several trance triggers, such as knocking on my altar three times or drawing the Maa Aankh, which was first outlined in detail in *Kamta: A Practical Kamitic Path for Obtaining Power,* and is discussed here in Chapter 4. You only need a few triggers and you can use whatever you want. The purpose again is to help you enter into a trance state so that you can work your spirit.

Forming an Intimate Relationship
With Your Superconscious and Subconscious

Remember that the same way suggestions made in the Alpha state like telling your ba what time you want to wake up, so that it instructs your sahu to follow your command, works. You can also give your ba simple commands to give your sahu regarding your physical body. For instance, whenever you have a slight pain in your body, understand that it is your sahu's way of indicating that something is out alignment. You can simply tell that part of your body to relax. If you were having a stomach ache you could tap your stomach and say "Settle down." Since the sahu is reactive, whenever we find ourselves becoming anxious or nervous because we are in an uncomfortable or unfamiliar situation, you can also use this method by tapping your chest or stomach and telling it to "Relax, everything will be fine." Your sahu remember is the child part of your being. Any suggestion made in Alpha state will have an influence on you such as telling your ba "Thank you for perfect health."

Using Symbols

When we keep in mind that the sahu is the child part of our being, then the simple things used to entertain a child can also be used to captivate the sahu, such as symbols. For instance, although the following exercise can be used with or without a candle of the appropriate color, since the flickering of the candle will assist in putting you into a trance state. By taking a candle of the desire color and carve into it a simple request using a toothpick or pin. Then rubbing it from the wick downward or to you for attracting something to you (if trying to rid yourself of something like a destructive habit or to sell your car, etc. bite or break the wick end to make it a base and reverse the candle. Then rub it from the base towards the wick away from you). Next create a simple chant with the using the appropriate color. For a more concise and detailed explanation on the use of colors and command terms see *Kamta: A Practical Kamitic Path for Obtaining Power.*

- Red – to remove obstacles chant "Clear!" "Conquer!" "Defeat!" "Protect!" and "Remove!" The color red can also be used to stimulate passion, which is the reason why it is commonly prescribed for love.
- Green – to increase one's happiness, improve relationships, friendships and love chant "Bless!" "Repeat!" "Refresh" and "Renew". Since the green is associated with growth, it would be the ideal color for those wanting children to wear. However, it wouldn't

64

in one's best interests if they were suffering from a debilitating illness like cancer to surround one with.

- Black – to create miraculous outcomes out of grim situations chant "Absorb!" and "Release!" It should be noted that there is no such thing as good and evil. Everything is neutral and can be used for either constructive or destructive purposes.
- White – to recover from an ill-ness, increase one's knowledge, understanding and wisdom chant "Enlighten", "Purify", "Balance!" "Bless!" and "Heal!". The color white can be used for many purposes and is considered a general use color.
- Pink – to remove stubborn and gloomy emotions chant "Clear!" and "Remove!" Pink can be used any time you are trying to overcome addiction, conquer negative energies with kindness, encourage harmonious relations, promote cleanliness and incite passion (not as fast as the color red).
- Purple – to control, dominate or master, while chanting "Assist!" "Chase!" "Drive!" "Break!" "Banish!" and "Destroy!" Can also be used with the color red. The color purple forces others to respect you because it is a royal color, once worn by high ranking officials.
- Orange – to create opportunities, change plans and perceive future events chant "Attract" "Direct!" "Draw!" "Focus!" and "Open!" Orange is a healthy dose of red and yellow, so a great color to help married couples work together harmoniously.
- Brown – to bring a sense of stability to one's physical plane and settle disputes especially legal matters chant "Balance!" Brown is a neutral color symbolizing the earth.
- Blue (Royal Blue) – to promote healing, create peace, joy and harmony chant "Expand!" and "Empower!"

- Blue (Pale Blue) – induce calmness and pleasant dreams.
- Light Blue – to create a feeling of tranquility, inspiration and devotion chant "Inspire!" and "Devote!"
- Yellow – to attract, invoke creativity, harmonize and imagine chant "Adapt!" "Bend!" "Center!" "Create!" "Chase Away!" and "Open!"

In the future chapters we explore how to make ritualistic use of all of these methods to make the process smoother, rhythmic, interactive and exciting.

Using Household Incense

Some herbs and spices have very good spiritual qualities that can be used. I learned how to use some of these from watching the old people in my family and Papa. These can be burned on incense charcoal or an open fire. When I am out of charcoal, I will burn them on the range or boil them in water to release its fragrance. It is not always as effective but, it is whatever works. Here's a listing of some:

Allspice also called Pimento is used for social occasions (not romance) to promote positive energies.

Bay Leaf also called Laurel is used to attract good luck and as the pun goes, "keep enemies at bay."

Cinnamon is one of the most powerful herbs in the house. A pinch of cinnamon burned with honey or brown sugar can be used to make any place loving and harmonious.

Coffee can be used a couple of ways. It has the ability to make one alert, which is why it is consumed so much in the western hemisphere. For this purpose it can be boiled and made into a strong tea for cleansing baths. The grounds can also be burned, which has an offensive odor that can ward off negative attacks.

Garlic Peels can be burned to clear the mind and also to bring about more food in one's home.

Honey can be burned on charcoal to sweeten an area. Brown sugar can be used the same way. You only need to burn a little honey or brown sugar.

Rosemary can be burned to ward off illness or made into a bath to attract money to one's home.

Rue is another strong household herb that can be used to ward off negative influences.

Tobacco particularly cigar smoke has a clearing effect wherever it is burned. Unlike cigarettes which have chemical additives, when tobacco is burned it sort of chases away negative energies and attracts positive ones. This is one of the reasons the Native Americans used it so much.

Using Herbs & Oils for Anointing

As I have mentioned previously, my family never used conditioned oils that are sold in novelty shops and curious stores, instead they've always used blessed virgin Pompeian olive oil, which was very green and hard a strong scent. I never asked what the significance was behind using this particular brand but I know that every house I went to during would use this same particular brand. When I learned the significance of using oils and herbs, I began using essential oils and if I couldn't get the oils, I would use the herb. I stay away from novelty items because I don't know who made the stuff. Here's a listing of the purpose and most common oils that I use:

For Attraction – use Frankincense, Geranium, Honeysuckle, Lotus, Mint, Olive oil, spearmint or wisteria to bring someone or something to you

For Dreams & Meditation – use Lilac, Lily, Magnolia or Saffron to receive answers in your dreams or via meditation.

For Happiness – use Bergamot, Five Finger Grass, Lemon Grass, Lemon or Lemon Peel, Violet or White Rose Lavender, whenever the energy appears to be low as a temporary fix

For Healing – use Camphor, Eucalyptus, Mint or Peppermint to attract healing energies and thoughts

For Jinxing – you never know but sometimes you may have to rid yourself or something of certain things or people. Use Cactus, Citronella, Four Thieves Vinegar or Patchouli to drive or repel unwanted energies. Do not dab on your hands.

For Spiritual Matters – use Balsam, Benzoin, Cassia, Frankincense, Myrrh, Rue or Sandalwood to attract spiritual energies especially when struggling with vices hindering you from growing spiritually.

For Love – use Almond, Cinnamon (to attract a woman), Clove (to attract a man), Coriander, Jasmine, Lotus, Mandrake, Myrtle, Orange, Vanilla, Vervain (Verbena) or Ylang Ylang to attract your soul mate, also good for social events.

For Luck Matters – use Anise, Cinnamon, Jasmine or Tonka Bean to get that extra boost. Only works if you have done all of your leg work first. Miracles only occur if you make preparations for them.

For Legal Matters – use Anise or Galangal for justice in the courtroom.

For Money Matters – sprinkle and/or anoint your money with Bayberry or Honeysuckle oil or herb. Since most people use plastic now and not cash, use to anoint your billfold, wallet and anywhere money is held.

For Peace – use Allspice, Germanium, Lavender, Lily, Orange, Sandalwood, Rose Geranium or White Rose to calm and soothes any atmosphere.

For Power & Domination – use Calamus or High John the Conqueror to help you obtain self-control, control a situation or to help you overcome anything or anyone.

For Protection – use Bergamot, Cayenne (or Red Pepper), Five Finger Grass, Lemon, Tobacco or Wintergreen to ward off negative energies and negative people. It helps to protect against spiritual and physical harm.

For Success – similar to luck herbs and oils, use Benzoin mixed with Cinnamon to helps you by boosting your confidence. Only works if you have done the legwork.

For Uncrossing – use Dragon's Blood, Nutmeg, Pine, Rue, Sassafras or Wormwood to remove negative influences. Anytime you feel that you have something on you, most of the time you do. Don't try to figure out how you picked up the negative energy. Use the following to remove it first.

Whenever I use the oils to anoint something I rub downward to get rid of something and rub upward to draw something to me. If I am using it on a candle, to draw the energy in I rub from the wick downward to the base. If I am repelling something then I turn the candle upside down, bite or break the end off to create a new base for the candle. Then I rub from the top downward. These are all symbolic gestures that the ba and sahu understand.

The way I anoint a thing is by taking a small dab of oil and vigorously rubbing my hands together to activate the oil. Since I am using an essential oil, it doesn't take much. In fact, you might want to dab a little olive oil in your hands if you have sensitive skin. If I am using the herb, I will simply dab a small amount of the powdered herb in my hand and pray over it. Then sprinkle or dust it over the things I am trying to anoint. When in doubt though, I always keep blessed olive oil in my house and use it for general purpose and sprinkle the powdered herb in my palms.

Another very quick way to perform an uncrossing is by using a white chicken egg. This was a practice I learned from a curandera (Latin American folk healer from the Curanderismo tradition). There are several ways to do this, but one of the simplest is just to pray asking that the negative energy be absorbed into the egg. The egg can then be broken or thrown away. I prefer to break to recognize that the energy was broken. Again, use your intuition.

Using Symbols for Amulets

Amulets and talismans are basically symbols used to communicate a certain idea to your ba and sahu. An amulet is basically an object that is worn, while a talisman is positioned in a fixed place like on a house, in the car, etc. Both can be anything and it can be made out of anything such as a piece of jewelry, a scripture copied down by a specific individual, an image, etc. because the effectiveness of it rests on what the owner of the tool believes. No, a crucifix itself doesn't ward off evil, but the idea it creates in the ba and sahu does and gives its wearer a feeling of protection.

In India, parts of Africa, Spain and Greece there is a belief in the notorious evil eye. Most people in western hemisphere don't believe it because they don't understand the science behind it. Simply put we in the States spend more time trying to comprehend why something works then accept that it does, which is good in a way because it allows us to understand a phenomenon from another perspective. Well, basically the evil eye, which is called Mal de Ojo, Malochio, etc. is an envious glance that cast upon someone or a thing. There are numerous theories as to how it is transferred, such as through the eyes as a continuous stare. While no one knows for sure how it occurs, what is known is envy is a real energetic force and it does affect us all on a subconscious level. The reason most don't believe in it is because 99.9% of the world population doesn't willingly wishes evil on another. We do so unconsciously.

Proof of this can be seen amongst individuals trying to outdo one another. For instance, have you ever found yourself hearing about the success of a family member, friend or associate, and for no reason at all, found yourself asking how come you can't have these same things? or asking, how could come the other individual was able to get these things and not yourself? These are all forms of the evil eye, because it affects us on a subconscious level.

This is why in Cuba for instance, to ward off the evil eye, people will paint an eye with a protruding tongue stabbed with a knife. The analogy it simple, the knife a symbol of protecting is used to communicate the idea stops all evil glances and slanderous tongues.

You can use any symbol you feel appropriate to create your own amulets and talismans. Whatever symbols you hold dear are the only ones that matter. For instance, if you believe an ankh symbolizes the protecting your life so be it. You can even make a pschent herst (the sacred white and red necklace discussed in Maa Aankh volume two). Whatever you decide understand that no one is in the position to tell you otherwise.

Crystals, Gems & Stones

Crystals, gems and stones belong in the previous section, but I wanted to give this section special attention because gems and stones can be used a number of ways. They can be carried in your pocket, worn in jewelry, placed in charm bags, added to your hets (altars and shrines, which will be discussed later), etc., because they are basically fossilized minerals and organic material.

We have to remember that everything has its own energy, which means that when you look, touch, etc. a thing. It makes you feel a particular way. Over time, it was learned that like oils, resins and herbs, certain crystal, gems and stones radiate a particular type of energy as well. The following is a list of some of the most commonly used and effective crystals, gems and stones[4]:

- Agate – has the ability of making one feel happy and peaceful during competition.

[4] Please note that in some traditions, crystals, gems and stones are directly associated with specific energies. I personally tend to not do this because subconsciously it creates a rule, which later evolves into a dogma. Like, quartz can't be added to anything with iron, etc. due to their astrological influences. I specifically use the Maa Aankh cosmogram and the Seven Codes of Maa, as my guides, and push all of the other theoretical stuff to the side.

- Amethyst – is a mauve or purple colored quartz crystal that gives one a protected feeling especially against negative energies. For this reason it is recommended that it be rubbed on one's forehead to remove headaches.

- Aventurine – is a basically a type of quartz that are available in a variety of colors. The green type inspires feelings of creativity. The blue stimulates feelings of inner strength. Red aventurine seems to create a feeling of luck and opportunity.
- The yellow variety creates a feeling of emotional stability.

- Bloodstone – is a green stone with deep red spots resembling blood, which makes one feel as if they are protected from the evil eye and circulation problems.

- Cat's Eye – also known as Tiger's Eye, Hawk's Eye and Falcon's Eye, stirs the emotions, thus creating the feeling of intense focus and keen observation.

- Coral – is the skeletal remains of aquatic polyps. Coral comes in a several colors but the most widely used is red Coral, which gives one the sense that they are protected from the evil eye and other forms of harm.

- Diamonds – are one of the most overrated gems of all, because initially they tended to bring peace to quarrelling parties. This is the reason it became the symbol used to represent the marriage between a man and wife.

- Emeralds – are green stones that tend to stimulate feelings of beauty.

- Garnets – are another one of those stones that comes in a variety of colors. The most prized are the reddish orange stones that inspire purity, understanding and stimulates business success.

- Jade – is an ancient green stone considered to many Chinese because it stimulated feelings of productivity, therefore money. Jade tends to work by strengthening one's mental faculties and assisting in decision makings.

- Jasper – is an interesting stone that comes in many colors but they all tend to work the same way, which is stimulating a feeling of protection from emotional stress and things that aren't good for you.

- Lapus Lazuli – was one of the most widely used stones in Kamit, because it made one feel like they were protected personally by the Divine. Lapus lazuli's deep rich and rare blue color also made one feel omniscient (all–knowing). For this reason it was commonly used in interpreting future events.

- Lodestones – are actually a form of magnetite that has a natural magnetic polarity. They are commonly used because they give the impression of attracting things to it.

- Moonstone – comes in a variety of forms, but the most powerful is the white moonstone, which enhances one intuition, thereby giving a feeling that one is protected and lucky.

- Opal – have you ever met or heard of any women named "Opal"? Usually they are rough character and it is probably because opals are considered the wild card of gemstones. There are various types of opals such as fiery opal, pink opal, etc. The most benevolent is the white opal, which makes one feel as if they have supernatural powers and can accomplish anything.

- Pyrite – is one of the most widely used minerals because it resembles gold. For this reason it is called, "Fools gold" because it makes one feel as if they are financially lucky. Pyrite also encourages one to overcome feelings of inadequacy.

- Quartz – is the most prized stone of all because it has the unique ability of making one feel cleansed and pure. It was commonly used in the Old Kongo to symbolize the knowledge and wisdom of the ancestors. There are a number of different types of quartz but the most efficient ones are amethyst, aventurine, girasol quartz (also called girasol opal) and crystal quartz. Crystal quartz gives one a feeling of inner peace and its ice like appearance cools tempers, thus allowing one to calmly and effectively end conflicts. Girasol crystal is a milky white or milky clear stone that has the tendency to do the same thing as crystal quartz, but also tends to give one a feeling of self – control over their impulsive behavior.

- Ruby – is one of the most popular stones because it is tends to stimulate feelings of power, protection and loyalty. Rubies come in a variety of colors from vermillion to red, but it's best to purchase rubies that are red or have a hint of blue in them giving them a purplish color. It is recommended that ruby rings because worn on the receiving hand or the left hand. Its reddish and purple tinge also has the tendency to inspire passion especially within men and courage in making difficult decisions. Like other stones associated with the blood, rubies also create the feeling that one is protected from germs and infections.

- Sapphires – are interesting stones that inspire peace, which stimulates mental clarity. They exist in a variety of colors but the best ones are the yellow sapphires followed by the bluish black variety.

- Topaz – is considered a sacred stone because it incites feelings of inner peace, thus protecting from over confidence. It also tends to inspire protection from all negative influences including accidents and untimely death.

- Turquoise – is one of the oldest stones used for protection because, its light bluish color seemed to invoke feelings of protection from all forms of violence. Since the color of turquoise tends to be associated with peace and wisdom. It was felt that it brought an end to any conflict, thereby bring good fortune and protection to whoever possessed it.

- Zircon – is another one of those stones that occurs in many colors or even be colorless. Looking more like a meteorite than a stone, zircon tends to encourage fame. It also inspires people to transform their life and strive to achieve meaningful goals.

There are numerous ways you can work with crystal, gems and stones. One of the simplest ways however, is to holding them in your hand and will your intent into them the way you do anything else. Before doing this, it is advised that you cleanse them by either placing them in sea salt water or blessed water.

The Kamitic Tablet Divination

Divination is not a sleight of hand. From a shamanic perspective divination is communication between one's ba, ab and sahu. When one approaches any oracle, rather they use a bible, stare at tea leaves, a bowl of water, coins, shells, cards, etc. it is their ab that is asking how to achieve a specific goal. The ba is providing the best possible solution to achieve the goal, while the sahu is inspired to pick, execute or throw a particular cast based upon past experiences, present feelings, etc. The conversation is as follows:

> Your *Ab* asks,
> "Is it in my best interest to trust so – and – so with my money?"
> *Ba* states, "Yes"
> *Sahu* recalls that you saved your money and you have done your homework on investments, so it is inspired to throw a particular cast that indicates "Yes" and if your tablets have been colored. It will inform you on how the success will manifest.

This particular divination system is practiced throughout Sub Sahara Africa, because it is simple and transportable. Like most divination systems it is not meant to dictate what one should and should not do, but to offer you further insight. For this reason it can be used to determine the truth of the matter, the end result of a decision, etc. I remembered one of the first times I used my tablets, there was a new company in town and they were offering all sorts

77

of incentives for people to come and work for them. At the time I was working for one company. They weren't bad but it was a job, so I asked "Would it be in my best interests to apply for a job?" The response was "No" with all of the tails turned up. A year later, the company closed because of mismanagement.

Head or Open Tablet

Tail or Closed Tablet

The tablet facing up is said to be the heads, while the back of the tablet symbols the tail. The head of the tablet is painted according to the four colors of Maa Aankh.

The tablet can be constructed using any manageable sized objects that can lay down flat on a flat surface, such as four coins of the same denomination, four pieces of wood of similar dimensions, four coconut rinds, four cowrie shells, etc. The tablets need to be painted yellow, black, red and white – the four colors revolving around the Maa Aankh. For a complete look at this divination system see *Maa: A Guide to the Kamitic Way for Personal Transformation.*

Once your tablets are ready, they need to be placed on a white saucer and baptized to consecrate them with you energy. To consecrate, anoint each with a few drops of water, olive oil spray them with rum and blow cigar smoke over them, which has a very purifying effect. You can then say a simple prayer that the tablets be blessed so that they can be used to help you reach your greatest potential and fulfill your destiny. Trust your intuition.

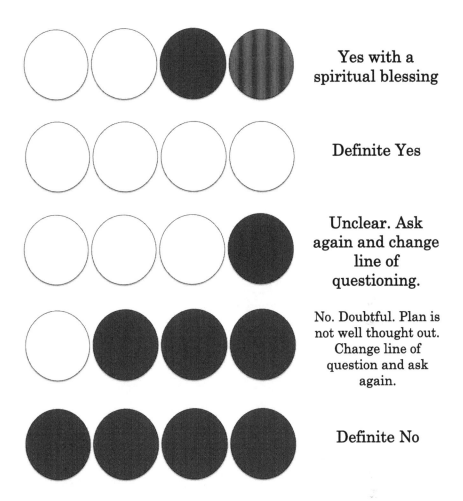

Yes with a spiritual blessing

Definite Yes

Unclear. Ask again and change line of questioning.

No. Doubtful. Plan is not well thought out. Change line of question and ask again.

Definite No

The basic rules of divination are never ask, the same question twice just because you don't like the cast. If you need to ask the question again, it is advised that you do it on another day assuming the outcome may have already changed. Second, never ask a question that you already know the answer.

To cast your tablets, you need a flat surface and a notebook to recorder the cast. To begin, hold your tablets in both hands. Raise them up towards the sky and then touch the center of your chest to symbolically connect your *ba* and *ab.* Next say a simple prayer like, "Speak through these tablets *Ba.*" This is a simple gesture meant to inform your sahu, that you are seeking a response from your ba.

Now, ask your question and formulate it so that it results in the most affirmative answer like "Is this the right time to ask for a promotion (pursue this business opportunity, change jobs, get married, etc.)?" or "Would it be beneficial for me now to accept this job offer (pursue a relationship with this individual, etc.)?"

While concentrating upon your question, throw your cast and record the pattern in your notebook. After you have recorded your reading, note and watch how the situation plays out. See how the advice offered by the reading comes into effect. Write the end results in your journal.

Chapter 3: Heroes of the Divine

As you have read from above, it you are relying only upon your sahu (the habitual and subconscious part of your being), you are not living up to your potential. You are not even using the full potential of your mind. You are in reality no different from a child. Actually a child is a little bit better off because they haven't been conditioned as to what to believe and not to believe. Understand I am not trying to insult you but get you to understand that we are all using one percent of our divine potential by living our lives based upon what our sahu tells us to do.

We need to access the other ninety – nine percent of our mind. The way to do this is by constantly holding in our mind's eye, clear, concise affirmative beliefs and thoughts, while imagining our desired end results. We see that by using our mind we can create any experience we want to have because our ba (superconscious or divine spark) mirrors whatever ideas and thoughts are in our ab – soul (conscious mind, soul or heart). This is the only thing we have to do. So the question is, why aren't more people healthy, prosperous, successful etc.?

Respect is Not Given, It's Earned

The reason more people aren't healthy, prosperous, successful, etc. is because if you will recall. The ab – soul (the conscious part of our being) is not in charge of our memories, but decision makings. The reason most people haven't been able to change their lives even after learning about the powers of the mind is because they forget that the ab – soul can't remember to do so. It has no real power. It has authoritative power but everyone that has ever worked a job knows that this power comes from others. Let me give you an example.

There is a popular saying that "Respect is not given. It is earned," which basically means just that, you have to earn respect and power. Just because you say your name, no one is going to drop down and treat you like a king or queen. Well, the same occurs within our being. Our sahu (subconscious self) has been running the show – that is our life – ever since we were babes. Then something extraordinary happened. All of sudden, we said when we became teenagers, "I don't want to do this anymore. I want to do that." And, as soon as we declared our will, the sahu part of our being felt threatened, so it rebelled. It rebelled because it was like, "How dare you tell me what to do." It didn't and still doesn't respect your ab – soul, just like when employees don't respect their boss, soldiers don't respect their commanding officer and so on. Does it make sense now why every time you affirm and declare your will, you have to prove it to yourself now? It is a fight between the selves.

The Big Me and the Little Me

The famous Italian opera tenor Enrico Caruso (February 25, 1873 – August 2, 1921) referred to this as the Big Me and the Little Me. According to the story, one night Caruso was suddenly struck with stage fright. Caruso claimed that all of a sudden his throat just became completely paralyzed because of his fear, which caused his throat muscle to spasm. Ashamed and trembling with fear, thoughts began to come to him that people would laugh at him because he couldn't sing. Behind the stage, he shouted to those near him that, "The Little Me wants to strangle the Big Me within." Out of defiance, he yelled, "Get out of here, the Big Me wants to sing through me."

I am sure you all have figured it out by now but, the Little Me that Caruso was talking about is of course our sahu, while the Big Me is our ba. It is said that Caruso continued to shout, "Get out, get out, the Big Me is going to sing!" When his name was announced, he proudly walked on to the stage and captivated his audience by singing.

We all have a Big Me and Little Me inside of us, because the conflict has always been within our mind – spirit. This same age old conflict has been described all over the world as the fight between good and evil. The Big Me and Little Me are described in the old Cherokee tale as the Good Wolf versus Bad Wolf. Of course good and bad are simply used to help explain how the classic masculine and feminine or positive and negative energies exist.

As you may have already guessed, the reason you understand the above allegories is because they are metaphors. Metaphors you will recall are one of the most ingenious methods used to bypass our sahu. To help aid in the process, using the *Story of Osar* as our guiding and instructional myth, Osar will be used to represent our Big Me, Good Wolf and our ba. Set will be used to represent our Little Me, Bad Wolf and sahu, while Hru will be used to represent our ab – soul.

Our Heroic Journey – The Evolution of the Soul

The world has been tricked into believing that mythological stories, legends and myths were fables told to entertain us as children. A lot of people never ask the question why the tradition of telling children scary stories before they go to bed existed in the first place. When we understand the nature of the human mind it becomes evident that the monsters in these mythological tales symbolize the monsters of our subconscious. The hero or heroine of the tale symbolizes our ab – soul (conscious) ability to triumph over the evil within. These stories were told by parents so that when the child falls asleep or encounters the boogey man that they would courageously fight in order to live the next day. In other words, it was a tool to teach children to overcome the fears and inhibitions of their lower self. This is the reason one of the most popular myths of all time is the Kamitic *Story of Osar.*

| Set (symbolizing our subconscious or physical body awareness, lower self, hence our Ego) | Hru (in Greek Horus the hero archetype symbolizing the our conscious mind and soul). | Osar (in Greek Osiris symbolizes our superconscious, higher Self or spirit) |

Figure 7: The Three Awareness

There are many versions of the story that exist because it changed to support every ruler, but the basis of the story always remained the same, which is that there were once two brothers, one-named Osar and his younger brother Set.

Story of Osar	**Commentary**
According to legend, Osar became king in a very horrific time, when his people were warring against each other. Wanting to bring peace to his land, Osar spoke with RA and asked him how he could bring peace to his people.	The word ra means ruler, power, etc. When compared to the Maa Aankh, Ra symbolizing the midday sun and waking consciousness is an allegory meaning Osar used reasoning.
Shortly after Osar found a solution, and he began teaching his people laws to govern themselves with.	This is an allusion to the fact that once an individual learns Maa (Absolute Truth). They look at every event from a cause and effect perspective, which eventually are grafted into law.
Osar taught his people agriculture, a trade he learned from his wife Oset. In a relatively short while the teachings of Osar had spread all throughout the land.	When one is truly divinely inspired, they see the importance of everyone, because everyone is significant and contributes to the whole. You don't have to force people to accept your way, because they can see it themselves.
Everyone loved Osar and cherished their beloved ruler except for his younger brother Set, who had become very jealous of Osar's success and fame.	This is an allusion to the fact that our sahu doesn't like anything new, so it will do everything in its power to avoid change.

85

Osar, seeing that everything was good, decided to spread his teachings throughout the world to help others.

In his absence, he decided to leave Oset in charge.

But, unbeknownst to Osar and Oset, Set was devising of a plan with several conspirators to murder his brother upon return.

When Osar returned back from his voyage, Set welcomed his unsuspecting brother and all the dignitaries of the kingdom with a great celebration.

When everyone was full and merry with ale, Set

Whenever someone discovers their maa (personal truth), naturally they want to share it with others in hope that it will align them with the Maa.

Those who discover the Divine for themselves know that the Divine is everywhere. They don't need dogma and threats of punishment issued to them to do right, offer their thanks and praise. They do so because they know their wellbeing is dependent upon it.

We always have to be forever diligent in what we hold in our awareness, because as they say, an idle mind is the devil's workshop.

The sahu knows us intimately, so it will always tempt us into reacting based upon our likes, dislikes and weaknesses.

When we keep in mind that the sahu is like a spoiled child that only wants to do

86

presented a beautifully decorated chest and promised to give it to whoever fit perfectly inside.

One by one, each of the guests tried to fit inside the chest, but no one could.

Set knowing all along that Osar would fit inside of the chest persuaded Osar to lie down in the chest, which he did, but before Osar was able to regain his stance.

what it likes and doesn't like, and its decision making is like that of a child. Whenever one is influenced or controlled by their sahu, the choices and decisions they make will appear foolish, silly, unwise, and just simply won't make any sense. This is why when people are intoxicated they do the stupidest things, but you don't have to be intoxicated to be manipulated by the sahu. Intoxication is just the extreme case.

The sahu craves attention and acceptance, so it will always try to make it appear that what it wants is the cool and the best thing to do because everyone else is doing it. Here lies the dangers of following the group and peer pressure.

The reason why we hesitate to do something is usually out of fear or uncertainty. It is a natural emotional response whenever we encounter unfamiliar circumstances or are placed in unfamiliar situations. Set knowing all along that Osar would fit inside the chest perfectly alludes to how our intellect can bring about our downfall.

Set and his conspirators nailed and poured molten lead on the chest.

It is in these moments, that our ba provides us with those first thoughts or cautions. Anytime the ba provides us with the idea to do something it usually corresponds to our personal experience. It is not going to contradict or conflict with what you believe, think or know.

As a result, Osar was suffocated and then Set had his conspirators throw the chest into the Nile to get rid of the evidence.

The suffocating of Osar is allusion referring to the suffocation of the ba or the suppression and drowning out the spirit. Where we ignore our intuition, inner voice, etc.

While this went on, no one opposed Set as he killed his brother and usurped the throne. Even Ra turns away while Set commited his horrendous acts of treason.

The sahu makes us feel like an outsider, but no one wants to go against the group. Ra turns away because according to the Maa Aankh, even though Set's actions are not justified, they are within aggression and reason.

When Oset heard what Set had done, she cut a lock of her hair and went into mourning. Wanting to give her dead husband a proper burial she put on her mourning clothes and went to find the chest containing the body of Osar.

Unable to find her, Set declared her Oset a fugitive.

Oset looked everywhere but could not find the chest anywhere. Then RA having pity upon her sent forth Npu (the Spirit of Opportunity, General Luck, Finder of Lost Things and Crossroads) to assist her.

Npu led Oset to a group of children, who told her that they saw the chest floating out towards the sea.

Guided by Npu, Oset boarded a ship and sailed out to sea where she came across a magnificent tree in

People, who know the Divine for themselves will always try to do what is Maa, regardless if it is popular or not.

The undying devotion that these individuals have towards the ba – spirit, leads them to creating miraculous change due to the thoughts that they entertain in their ab – soul.

Children are the physical manifestation of the Spirit Npu, because they symbolize the new ideas from the ba, which is how they were able to provide Oset with a new approach and direction.

This is an age old prophecy regarding the Maa, which indicates that whenever one loses knowledge of the

89

present day Syria. The tree was so beautiful that the king of the land had it cut down and made into a pillar, unaware that the chest of Osar was engulfed inside. After pleading with the king, the pillar containing the chest was opened and was returned to Oset.

On her way back to Kamit to give Osar a proper burial, overcome with grief. It is said that Oset opened the chest and through magical means caused Osar's member to impregnate her. Another version however states that she transformed herself into a swallow and encircled the body of Osar. Her wind caused by the flapping of her wings caused his member to rise and impregnate her.

Later the pregnant Oset hid the body of Osar in a marsh, while she stole away to a nearby town to birth Osar's heir Hru.

While away, Set, during a

ba. In dire times, they will rediscover it in distant lands.

In either case, the immaculate conception is the first attempt to explain how one's strong determination and will emerge.

The enemy doesn't like

hunting expedition, found the chest and, in a rage of anger, hacked up the body into 14 pieces.

When Oset returned and found what Set had done, she immediately went in search of the body Osar again, but this time her sister, Nebhet accompanied her. Everywhere they found a piece of Osar's body. They collected it and built in its absence a shrine.

When all of the body parts were collected except for the phallus, which was swallowed by a sacred fish. Together Oset and Nebhet along with Npu and Djahuti wrapped the body and mummified their king in order to give him a proper burial.

When the child Hru finally came to age, he had a dream from his father instructing him to avenge his wrongful death and reclaim his inheritance.

unity, so it always tries to conquer by creating division.

The shrine is a metaphor for practices; rituals and traditions used to bewilder the sahu, while at the same time empower the ba. Remember the sahu is habitual and is fond of symbols, metaphors, etc. This is the reason preaching and sermonizing doesn't have a long term effect, because the concepts are being impressed upon the mind – spirit.

The collected body parts of Osar symbolizes a whole system (literally and figuratively) that have unified and buried within hidden in order to prevent them from ever being lost again.

All it takes is for us to experience one miracle for us to realize that the divine spark is within. Once we do, we will diligently work to incorporate the divine in our life.

Hru choosing to follow his father's wishes challenged Set for the throne, but his valiant efforts only led to him winning a few battles, because Set was stronger and had more experience. In one decisive battle he proved this by gouging out Hru's eye causing the young prince to barely escape with his life.

Hru fled to his father's old vizier Djahuti who repaired his eye perfectly. When Hru engaged Set again on the battlefield he defeated his uncle and managed to castrate him.

Hru dragged his uncle before Oset, so that she could pass judgment on him, but Oset refused to sentence Set to death citing that he was family. Afterwards, she chose to free Set from his bondage.

This is where we see that life is not about right or wrong, or what is fair but about spiritual power. You will never be able to defeat your enemy by relying solely upon natural means.

Djahuti symbolizes the wisdom of the ba, which gives one perfect insight into how to resolve any problems. The castration is an allusion to the sahu's passions. Remember, the sahu functions primarily on likes, by castrating Set, it limits his emotional control over us.

When it is understood that without evil you can't have good, and without negative you can't have a positive. It becomes clear that our sahu symbolized as Set is the divine opposition created to make us strive for fulfillment. Without opposition we would not be

92

who we are today.

It wasn't long after Set was free; he began spreading lies and tried to discredit Hru claiming that he was not the legitimate heir of Osar.

This is also a reminder that we cannot take a passive approach when it comes to our salvation, because our habitual self will take advantage of any weakness, hence an idle mind is the devil's workshop.

Eventually the matter was brought before a tribunal and both Set and Hru presented their case, but the judges could not come to a consensus as to who was the rightful heir to the throne of Osar. Then finally, Djahuti who was knowledgeable of the mysteries made way for the deceased Osar to speak. When Osar spoke he reminded the tribunal that he was the one that brought teachings, laws and agriculture to the land. The tribunal noting that Set during his reign did not reproduce Osar's efforts, declared Hru to be the true heir. Hru was crowned with the white and red Pschent crown symbolizing the unification of the land.

There are many truths that can be drawn but the most important one is that one's truth reflects in their daily life. As we saw in the previous chapter, your dominant thoughts manifest themselves physically and this is why Set was found to be a hypocrite. There are many people that claim to believe in one thing but do the complete opposite. Hru was said to be *maakhru (maaxeru)*, true of his word because his actions mirrored his thoughts (words). The crown therefore symbolized the unification of his upper and lower spirit.

And, everything that Set
destroyed of his father, Hru
rebuilt in Osar's honor.

When you read the story without the commentary you
will receive great insight into other areas of your life, but I
chose to focus on how the *story* relates to our mind – spirit so
that you can see the story is about fighting our lower self –
sahu. This whole journey can all be illustrated using the
following diagram.

The Journey of Hru & Good versus Evil

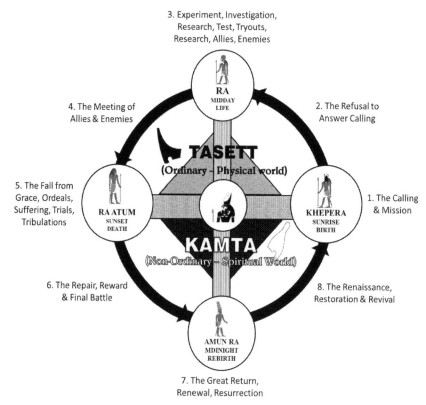

Figure 8: The Kamitic Hru's Journey

Understand that this is not by any means saying that you are supposed to go through life without any feelings or experiencing any likes or dislikes. Quite the contrary, what this means is that you are not supposed to allow your anxieties, fears, guilt, worries, dictate and tell you how to live your life. When you experience an emotion, as a child of the Divine made in the image of God, you are supposed to use that emotion to create change. Not cower. This is the reason a lot of theologians avoid commenting on Genesis 1:26 because although it says they are made in the image of God. They have allowed their earthly experience to dictate how they should live. If you believe you are a child of God, as soon as you hear that people in your community don't have jobs and it is predicted that crime will rise.

You should be working to create a miracle and bring jobs to your community. Why? Because you are a child of God and God has and knows no limitations. Your divine birthright is that you have the power to overcome any conditioning. Loss, misfortune, problems, obstacles, trials and tribulations are the Creator's way of purifying our soul of negative attributes of the Spirit, so that we can a true sense of fulfillment. This means technically speaking there is no such thing as good and evil. This is a maa (our personal or subjective truth) concept that human beings created in order to better understand ourselves and the universe around us. The concept of good and evil is not Maa (Absolute Truth). If it were, then every positive force would be considered good and every negative force would be considered evil, but we know that hot water is not good and cold water is evil, or vice versa. Both have to exist in for the other to exist, which is balance or Maa.

Just like light and dark. Light is not good and the darkness is evil. In fact, if you have too much light you can still experience blindness, whereas in a dark room you can

95

still see if you use your senses correctly. Are you starting to get the picture?

Basically, the same way we have to balance fire in order to cook our food because too much fire and the food will burn, but if we don't apply enough fire. It will not thoroughly cook our food for our body's nourishments. We have to do the same thing with every other element on our planet.

Good and evil is not some eternal battle occurring between God and his much less powerful creation, the devil for control of our soul. It is an internal battle that has been going on for ages within man and woman for domination of our conscious mind and our destiny.

If you don't accept and understand that both God and the devil are within you, then you will always live your life not truly knowing what is right from wrong based upon a subjective truth, and being easily manipulated by others who claim to have your best interest into doing things including harming others because they don't share the same beliefs and ideas as you. We have to remember that the true devil is a deceiver and is a wolf hiding in sheep clothing. The devil has convinced everyone that he is red hoofed man with the head of a goat running around sticking people with his pitchfork. This is simply not true. This image like most mythological images was meant to symbolize the devilish forces that exist in our sahu.

When we look at all the atrocities committed in the name of religion we have to realize that this was not God ordained, but authored by the devil or Set within. This is the reason the Kamitic sages went through so much effort to teach others their spiritual tradition by inscribing and advertising it on the wall, so that their citizens and others inspired by them would never forget that they are a true expression of the Divine.

Understand. You are a divine being. A microcosm of a greater Macrocosm and the only one that doesn't want you to remember this is your lower self because he doesn't want you to change. This is why the best way to remind yourself of your divinity and that your outer world is a reflection of your inner world – thoughts, beliefs, ideas, etc., is to think of your entire being as a mini-kingdom. Where your sahu (the habitual subconscious part of your being) corresponds to your physical body awareness, all physical things, etc. and represented as TASETT ruled by Set who appears on your left shoulder.

However, deep within your ba (the intuitive and omnipotent part of your being) corresponds to your spiritual or divine awareness and is represented as KAMTA ruled by Osar who appears on your right shoulder. But we cannot err in our thinking as has been done in the West and believe that one is good and the other is evil.

This is the reason for simplicity purpose the Kamitic sages often associated these concepts to the Eyes of Ra. To remind us that we need both (the so-called good and evil or Osar and Set) in order to have a holistic, complete, well rounded, balance view of life. The question is who will you allow to rule you? Will you allow your uncle Set to be your guide in life or your father Osar?

The Sahu
(Habitual Subconscious)

Aakhut: The Right Eye of RA
(Solar Eye) [5]

Set

The Ba
(Intuitive
Superconscious)

Aabit: The Left Eye of RA
(Lunar Eye) [6]

Osar

---

[5] The Aakhut or right Utchat (Eye of Ra) represents information controlled by the left hemisphere of the brain such as factual information, letters, numbers, words, aggressiveness, masculinity, the sun, the living, etc.

[6] The Aabit or left Utchat (Eye of Ra) represents information processed by the right hemisphere of the brain such as abstract ideas, dreams, esoteric thinking, feelings, intuitive thoughts, receptivity, femininity, the moon, ancestors (or spirits), etc.

Lesson 3:
Becoming Consciously Superconscious & Overcoming Your Fears

In the previous lesson we learned how to form an intimate relationship with our ba and our sahu because many people believe that their superconscious mind (higher self, God, etc.) is outside of them or beyond their reach. Quite the contrary, it is within you and has been within you since the beginning. Presently, you are functioning from your ba, but you aren't aware of it because of how you identify with your sahu or lower subconscious spirit. So, in this lesson we will focus on helping you to shift your ab – soul's conscious awareness to help you to consciously be superconscious. This is not something that is going to occur instantaneously where all of a sudden you are going to wake up and be a different individual, but through regular practice it become a lot easier to shift to this state of being.

Personalizing Your Superconscious and Subconscious

Since we live in a society where everyone thinks that they are not good enough and they are constantly focusing on self-improvement. People want to be a better salesperson, a better speaker, perform better at this and that, because they see themselves as a flawed and sinned individual. In Kamitic spirituality, human beings are not seen as being a sinned creature but a divine being that has acquired some gross impurities. In other words, we are gods and goddesses that have fallen; now we are trying to rise back up. That's right. If the idea of the fallen angel Satan came to mind, it is because we are all Set. We all have something we struggle with because it is part of this experience. It is important however to understand that this is part of the transformation. The thing that we struggle with is in our life in order to help us to build character and see our divinity.

To communicate with your Osar and Set, go into KAMTA and think about the times when you become anxious, fearful, worrisome, depressed, jealous, etc. Now imagine Set and tell yourself that whenever you feel these emotions these are all signs that your Set is speaking. Next, think of what it means to be all knowing, wise, compassionate, loving, powerful, truthful and peaceful. Once you have done this see yourself dressed in white wearing the white Hedjet crown of Osar. Begin to associate all of your benevolent experiences with the Hedjet crown or Osar.

Recognizing When Are You Superconscious

It is easier to recognize when you are in KAMTA than it is when you are, because KAMTA is peaceful, serene and magical. It is so full of wonder that it is easy to recognize when you are not identifying with Osar because it will appear unnatural.

So, whenever you are not feeling well within and whenever you feel like things are not working out right, you are not identifying with your Osar. Whenever you find yourself arguing with yourself, arguing or discussing something with another or going back and forth on if you should doing something or not, you are not identifying with your Osar. When nothing seems to be happening right and when everything seems to be going wrong, you are not identifying with your Osar but with Set.

You are identifying with your Osar whenever you feel really good and satisfied within yourself. When everything you seem to do seems to be right on time or everything is happening just right. When you identify with your Osar,

100

when working with another there is no argument because you are speaking to the core of their being, so you speak and hear what was said. You don't force another to accept or believe what you are saying. When you identify with your Osar you are calm, cool, and peaceful and focused on the present not worried about the past or the future.

Being in KAMTA is not about trying to get something, because you are identifying with your Osar right now. Being in KAMTA is just about being in a calm, peaceful, worry – free, fearless state of being. Remember, any time you fear anxious, guilt, fear, worrisome, unhappy, overly stressed, upset, etc. you are being pulled out of your KAMTA state of being.

Overcoming Anxieties, Fears and Worries Forever

Most of the time we are thrown out of our natural KAMTA state is whenever we encounter anxiety, fear and worry. Most peoples' fears are totally imagine and are based upon the subconscious programming in their sahu. The following Arabian tale demonstrates this:

> Pestilence met a caravan on the road to Baghdad. The caravan leader asks, "Why are you making such haste to Baghdad Pestilence?"
>
> Pestilence responded, "To take five thousands lives." On the way back, the caravan leader met Pestilence on the side of the road and exclaimed, "You lied. You took not five thousands lives, but fifty thousand!"
>
> Pestilence replied, "No, I did not. I took only five thousands lives, Fear took all the rest."

It is quite natural for us to fear the unknown. If you came across a wild animal, it is natural for your sahu to go into the whole fight or flight response. This is one of the ways that our sahu helps us to survive, which is when encounter something that is new and strange, we are supposed to approach it with caution and a bit of skepticism. This is called a justifiable fear and the way to deal with this type of fear is address the issues you fear. My suggestion would be to first take several deep breaths to relax yourself and do the obvious things in dealing with your concerns.

For instance, say that you want to buy a used car but you are afraid of getting scammed because you don't know too much about cars. This is a justifiable fear of the unknown. What you do is take a breath and relax. Then take the car for a test drive and to a mechanic or someone who knows cars. Pay them to check the car out thoroughly. You can also check the Blue Book price. If you don't know what this is, the mechanic should know and since you are paying them. They should help you out.

Most justifiable fears are in your control. They consist of concerns and issues where the obvious thing you need to do is acquire the proper knowledge. If you fear drowning because you don't know how to swim, obviously learn how to swim, and so on.

Then there are those other fears that we have which is the result of anxiety. A student knows the answer to a particular problem on an exam but his or her mind goes blank out of fear of failure. I have witness for myself having the knowledge to accomplish anything, and then all of a sudden mess up. We have all heard or read of young adults who receive a pretty lucrative athletic contract only to fumble it away because of some silly antic. It all stems from fear of failure.

There are several ways of overcoming these types of fears. The fear of failure is rooted in the emotional energy anxiety. When a fearful thought comes to you suggesting that you are going to fail or you will not succeed. Simply imagine the greatest benefits you will receive if you are successful. The forgetful student for instance might imagine the joy he or she will have in making an "A" mark on the examination. A student athlete with a lucrative contract may want to imagine being congratulated by his or her elders on a job well done. This might help in causing the athlete to consider his or her public actions and behaviors, and so on.

There are other fears that stem from worry of the future based upon the past. These fears we may not have direct control over but we can control how they influence our life by issuing an affirmative suggestion. No one knows when setting out on trip if they are going to encounter a crazy driver, an accident, etc. Those who understand the power of suggestion know that they don't need to worry because they can project or speak a blessing preventing it. The theory is that you cannot always control what happens around you, but you can control how you choose to respond to it.

Before setting out on a trip, bless yourself or declare a blessing that you will go and return safely. It has to be an affirmative blessing that will allow you to see the end result. I remember when I became ill and could not walk, I blessed legs to dance, so that I would be able to eventually walk and run.

I learned from Papa that in Cuba there are all sorts of blessings done to address this fear, such as blessings spoken over the family, blessings spoken over the home, blessings spoken over the doors, etc. Blessings can be said over anything and everything*. They can be made up or come

103

from a reputable source. This is the reason Psalms 23 is so popular in the African American community. It also is the basis of such folk practices as saying a prayer over your food before eating.

As you may have already figured out, fear causes us to sabotage our best efforts. The way to overcome fear is to address it from the superconscious perspective, which isn't afraid of anything. So, whenever you have a fear, always check to see if it is justified. If so, do something about it. If you are afraid of the repercussions from a poor diet, then you need to adopt a better and healthier lifestyle. If you cannot afford a membership at a, fitness center or to hire a personal fitness trainer, project the end result of what you want and allow your ba and superconscious to work out the details. These small little hurdles is what stop us the most from achieving our greatest success, but we have to remember our job is not to figure out how to make something work – that's the purpose of the ba and sahu. Our job is to decide on what we want and do it.

If the fear is a fear of failure, project what you could accomplish if you were to succeed instead. Keep this image in your mind and daydream on it as much as possible.

Finally, speak an affirmative blessings based upon your desired end result, over that part of your life that you fear. You can either speak this aloud or repeat silently (i.e. I am beautiful. I am confident. I am serene, and so on) as mentioned in the previous lesson, to sow the idea firmly into your spirit.

* Note that you can combine these methods for addressing your fear with the methods and techniques described in the previous chapter. For instance, to protect your door from intruders, bless your door with blessed olive oil that can be

104

placed on the outside (outside facing towards the street), or on the door handles. This works great against pesky solicitors.

Embracing the Pain

There's a moment in our lives when we reach what I call the bottom. It is the point where you have taken all that you can take and can't take anymore. It's the moment where you have simply had enough. It's the tipping point, the breaking point where your emotions are so raw you could burn a thing with your eyes. This moment or point is what I call the end of your humanity. It is the point that society has suppressed and has made you feared. You're afraid that if you tap into this raw power that you are afraid of what you would do. Well, that's a load of crap! This is the true you that you are hiding.

When you can't look a person in the eyes, you feel your chest caving in or butterflies in your gut. It is because this is an unconscious response to you living in fear and not being free.

If you want to be free, you have to do what I call embrace the pain. Remember, our sahu (subconscious self) does not like pain, in fact loathes pain and looks for the easy way out of everything. This is why it is easier to look away from the individual that harms and disrespects you, and then you end up hating yourself later. In order to be consciously superconscious and free, you have to embrace the pain because when you embrace the pain. You force self to remember so that whatever happened in the past will never occur again. When an individual that embraces the pain they are pissed! And, when they are pissed off, they don't care what others think because they are pissed. When an individual embraces the pain, instead of ignoring it, they aren't pissed at the world. They are just pissed at a specific situation.

Recall embarrassing situations where you were ridiculed out of fear. Think about the job you could have and how you would have been paid more, if you just would have applied. Think about the relationship bliss you could have had if you just would have expressed how you felt and trusted your intuition. You can't get upset with others who overcame their fears to rise to the occasion. You can only get angry with the fact that you surrendered to your fears. So, the next time your fears rise up. Look at what you will gain instead of what you will lose. Then, go forward.

Chapter 4: Reclaiming Your Blessings

Before proceeding I must remind you that the whole purpose of this heroic adventure from a Kamitic perspective is to bring your ba – the divine spirit or higher self, symbolized as Osar – out of dormancy or to the forefront, so that it can play a more active and prominent role in your life. When you begin to see life from a divine perspective, you'll see that there several realities that exist alongside each other, in other words, they are parallel realities.

Parallel Realities

You see right now, most of us rely upon our ba only in times of crisis. We for the most part function from a reactive consciousness. Whereas we wait for 'drama' or events to occur then we want to cry out for help. We need to have a proactive consciousness whereas instead of waiting for events to unfold so that we can respond to them. We think about it, and then act before the event occurs. Many of us are proactive when it comes to the seasonal changes. We know for instance, that winter is on its way so we take vitamins and take out winter clothing in preparation for the cold season. We just need to be this way in regards to our daily living by keeping in mind that our sahu – the physical body consciousness or our lower self, symbolized as Set – makes us respond impulsively and instinctively with anger, anxiety, envy, frustration, greed and the like. When however we choose to be proactive our Osar allows us to respond by being charitable, compassionate, joyful, optimistic and serene. Every moment, as Children of Osar, we are given the opportunity to choose to follow our father Osar and be proactive or our uncle Set and be reactive. Each time we resist the trappings of Set and follow our Osar even if it is as simple as greeting a neighbor, holding the door open for a stranger or giving a person on the street spare change. We are able to improve the quality of our life because it makes our ba that much stronger.

While it is impossible to plan and know when an event is going to occur like the preparation for the winter season. We can prepare in advance how we choose to react and respond to a given situation by shifting our awareness. In fact, studies have found that when people switch their personality, their brain wave patterns and their capacity also shifts. Dr. Bennett Braun, of the International Society for the Study of Multiple Personality[7], in Chicago, reports how one of his patients was generally allergic to orange juice would break out into painful hives even after taking the smallest of sips. However, when one of the patient's personalities named Timmy was in control, the man could drink as much orange juice as desire with no allergic reaction at all. What was even more astonishing was that whenever the other personalities were present, the man experienced the same painful allergic reaction but as soon as the Timmy personality took control, the hives quickly faded[8].

Think about that for a minute. Imagine you have several personalities or ways you can respond to an event or situation. There is a side of you that doesn't know anything, but there is also a side of you that is all knowing. For

---

[7] From an ancient shamanic perspective we all have numerous personalities. The difference between us and those suffering from the multiple personality psychological disorder, is that we have the ability to choose, which personality we want to manifests, whereas the latter lacks the conscious will or ability to do so.

[8] Goleman, Daniel (1988, June 28). Probing the Enigma of Multiple Personality. New York Times.

instance, say you want to learn how to speak a foreign language. Well, there is a personality that doesn't know how to speak a foreign language. Then on the flip side there is a personality that is fluent in speaking multiple languages. So essentially when we are proactive we are tapping into a parallel reality, which is like turning the channel to tune into another frequency.

What this means is that Osar and Set represents dual realities. The proactive conscious of Osar is an emotional state of order, while the reactive conscious of Set is a chaotic emotion. In other words, if you are having financial difficulties in your life – you are experiencing the reactive Set side or chaotic state, then know that on the flipside there is a "you" that is not having financial difficulties or experiencing Perfect Finance – the proactive Osar side or peaceful state. Perhaps you have a personality that is a perfect artist but there is another that has no interest in art at all. At the same time, those of us experiencing perfect state should know that its polar personalities are near. For instance, those of us experiencing Perfect Health also have harboring within us a personality that is ill.

The point is that we don't always know why we are in a particular situation or why something is occurring, but we can either choose to be reactive or proactive, or be the victim or the victor by shifting to another personality. The way we choose to be the victor is by taking responsibility for our actions and behaviors instead blaming it on others or external events. Once we do this with the understanding that there is no such thing as good and evil. We are reminded that obstacles, problems, trials and tribulations help to bring our Osar to the forefront.

That being said, have you ever asked yourself why there are so many problems in the world? Why do we have to struggle? Why do we have problems? Why do we have setbacks, obstacles, trials and tribulations? Why isn't life fair? Well, it is because like Hru we have to fight for our birthright.

Fighting for Your Birthright

This is a little hard to imagine especially if you are just beginning to get knowledge of Self. This is why I like to think of our birthright as being like a treasure room full of everything you ever wanted and could imagine. You imagine it, it is there and all you have to do is go over and pick up whatever it is you see.

Now imagine all of a sudden the lights in this room are turned off and it is pitch black. You know that everything that you ever wanted is in this room. The problem is that you can't physically see it. In order to get the thing that you want, you have to feel around in the dark and hope you find it.

The spiritual realm is like being in a brightly lit treasure room, whereas the physical realm is like being in a dark room. In the physical realm, you are limited by your physical senses, which is the reason we have so many problems in TASETT.

Who Turned Off the Spiritual Lights?

Well, the answer is that we all did, we just don't remember doing so. You and I both turned off the lights to our treasure or inheritance as soon as we decided to be born into this physical reality. The problem that most of us have is that we forgot the reason why we turned off the lights in the first place.

Why Did You Turn Off Your Spiritual Lights?

Well, you and I both turned off the lights because when the Divine showed us the treasure room on the other side, before we decided to be born. Our Creator told us afterwards that we were now the rulers of the Universe so govern it perfectly. Even though we were perfect beings created by a perfect Creator, we had no practical experience in how to do with God asks. It was like starting a new job at a fortune 500 company where our boss or supervisor gave us a tour of the entire corporation. Afterwards, our new boss showed us this treasure room and told us that all of the objects within it were accumulated over a period of time. They explain how they built their corporation from the ground up and their treasures are the prize possessions that reflect their success. Then, with no explanation, the boss simply says, "You're the boss now, so manage the corporation perfectly, because I am going on vacation."

Can you imagine the anxiety, the fear, worry and feeling of being overwhelmed that would overcome an individual given this news? Without any training, our boss simply tells us, "You are the boss now!"

So we asked the infinite wise and Almighty Creator to formulate a way so we could learn and master our skills in order to govern the Universe. We wanted to earn it, because we felt that if we didn't earn it, we wouldn't appreciate it. In response to our request, the Divine created the Universe and set obstacles in our path so that we could develop our skills and talents. It is through this physical experience we learn how to be selfless, forgiving, patient, studious, peaceful, optimistic, trustworthy, and all of the other divine attributes of the Spirit.

This is the reason individuals that survive debilitating illnesses become the best healers. Those who suffer great financial loss are able to amass great fortunes after learning how to properly manage their money. On the flipside, it also indicates that the reason so many of us whenever we come into an unexpected financial boon, shortly afterwards lose it because subconsciously we feel that we didn't earn it. Understand, it is not that we are sinned or don't deserve to be happy, healthy, rich, etc. No. It is that subconsciously we feel like we don't deserve them, so in order for us to be healthy, peaceful, patient, prosperous, you name it – whatever divine attribute it is – we have to earn it. Once we earn it, we coming into the KNOWING.

Why Is It Important to Know versus to Believe?

Again, why is it important that we come into our KNOWING? Because when you KNOW a divine attribute, nothing in the Universe can make you believe or think

112

different. You see, although we have talked extensively about being made in the image of the Divine and having divine attributes because we are all spiritual beings within a physical body with a soul. It is all theory or really idle talk that sounds good and makes sense. For some of us, it makes a great conversation around a coffee table, but for most of us because we are dominated by our subconscious sahu symbolized as Set. This idle talk becomes a theory that lays the foundation for a religion. Religion remember, is a system of control where one is instructed (usually out of fear) by an individual (or group of individuals) on how to live. Religion we have seen throughout the history of the world is typically anti-Spirit because it creates division amongst people based upon superficial differences like race, age, social status, gender, color, etc. It is important to understand that all religions begin with a fantastic and glorious beginning, but like all manmade things, they eventually degenerate because they are static whereas the ba – spirit is dynamic.

Spirituality is different in the sense that it creates a complete change in consciousness because it is not based upon belief but upon knowing. A person that overcomes a debilitating illness has no doubt in his or her mind how they were able to achieve it. They will tell anyone and everyone the same prescription they used and it will always centers on the same thing – divine intervention through personal determination.

So this is the reason for knowing and eventually we all want to get to the point where we have this knowing about everything such as knowing how to heal your body and others as well. Imagine knowing how to make a million dollars, knowing how to be successful, knowing how to improve any relationship, etc. This would be great wouldn't it?

Of course, but this means that in order for us to come into the KNOWING we have experience what it feels like to not know, hence the purpose of Set. This means that every time you experience an obstacle, setback, trial, tribulation, etc. You like Hru are experiencing this ill fate, so that you can travel to KAMTA, the mysterious Black Lands, the land of your Osar (your father, mother and collective ancestral land/memories) – in order to acquire true knowledge and wisdom, so that you can solve the problems of the world.

So the purpose of this heroic adventure we call life is to bring our ba or superconscious out of dormancy or poetically and metaphorically speaking, it is meant to resurrect your Osar, so that he (or she because the spirit is androgynous[9]) can play a more active role in your life. This means that in truth there is only one religion and it is really about learning how to control your mind. Although there are numerous ways to accomplish this, the ancient African shamanic way to achieve this goal, is by calling for some assistance from the forces that exist beyond our normal control. We call these forces, spirits.

What Are Spirits?

To understand what spirits are we have to first recognize that the Almighty Creator is an Infinite Spirit who created a host of beings with no physical form, that we call spirits. From an African shamanic perspective, our universe is full of nothing but spirits and the major difference between them and us is that we have a physical body whereas spirits do not. Spirits are therefore willful sentient (emotional) beings that exist throughout the universe. I know that definition is probably not what you want to hear but bear with me

---

[9] This is true meaning of godhead spirits like the Yoruba Obatala having male and female aspects.

because our universe is very mysterious and spirits rank right up there alongside it.

Since the beginning we have talked about how we are spiritual beings. We have talked about how our sahu corresponds to our subconscious self or "lower spirit" and our ba corresponds to the superconscious part of our being or our "higher spirit". We have also mentioned how both our ba and sahu governs our memories, and whenever we recall a memory, what we are actually doing is brining that entire experience back into the present moment. What this means is that spirits can be thought of as being infinite intelligences connected to the Source of Intelligence or the Divine.

Your ability to understand this will depend upon the perspective you take. It should be noted that most people will view spirits (angels, demons, gods, goddesses, saints, martyrs, daemons, demigods, etc.) as being outside of them, because this is how the early Christians saw God and all spiritual beings. Consequently, they viewed all spiritual entities as being superior over human beings. When the Roman Catholic Church became the official religion throughout Europe, it dominated the world by creating a religious schism whereas; if you weren't a Christian then you must have been a pagan who was in league with the devil. This furthered the misunderstanding about spirits, which is why I am choosing my words wisely and stating again. That spirits are willful sentient (emotional) beings that exist throughout the universe.

To get an idea what I mean by willful sentient beings or finite intelligence connected to the Infinite Intelligence or the Divine, imagine that your ba – the superconscious part of your being is like a grand library. Like most libraries, it is divided up into sections, categories, fiction and nonfiction, etc. Basically, each section is what our ancient ancestors

115

referred to as a spirit (angels, demons, gods, goddesses, saints, martyrs, daemons, demigods, etc.). Each subcategory was a sub-spirit and so on. Are you still with me? Good. Hang on because this is where it gets fun and you get to see superconscious magic work.

Remember, our ba and our sahu doesn't forget anything. Right now if you were to put this book down and walk away from it. Five minutes later you most likely wouldn't remember what you were reading or what page you left off on (unless you marked it) because, it is our ab – soul, the conscious part of our being, that doesn't have a very extensive memory. So if you want to remember what page you stopped on. You would have to thumb through the pages until you find a familiar passage, right? But, how do you remember events that took place last week? What about events that took place last month or a few years ago? Ok. What about events that took place before you were born or to another individual hundreds of years ago whom you may or may not be related to by blood. How would you recall any of this information? Obviously, your ab – soul couldn't but the information still exists within your ba – sahu spirit because they never forget anything. All it takes is the right conditions, the right situation, the right symbol, etc. to allow you to thumb through the memories of time so that you can find your place and this is where superconscious magic works at its best. Let me give you an example.

One day I got a hunch to offer my netchar Npu (whom you will meet here shortly) some seasoned palm oiled popcorn, rum, a red candle, pipe tobacco and sugar water for something I wanted. I left the offering in front of his image so that he and the lower spirits that work with him) could consume the energy of the offering. After the candle had burned all the way down, I closed the door to the room and went about my business. The next day, I got on the computer. I forgot that I was going to have company later on so; I started to straighten up around the house after I ate a little breakfast. Then, suddenly I got a phone call from my best friend in Detroit. We talked for about an hour or more, and then I went back to working on the computer. I forgot what I was working on but the question came up, "What are spirits?" I knew what they were but I wanted a specific way of writing it, and a book I had read came to mind. So, I had to go to my backroom. When I entered, I was reminded by the smell of the palm oil scented popcorn, the pipe tobacco, the rum and burnt wax, that I had given Npu an offering the other day.

This immediately triggered a memory and led me to another book dealing with a similar subject but from another culture. I was then reminded how the smell of popcorn makes me feel and how scents trigger certain memories. In less than a second, I got a glimpse of some ancient Africans categorizing certain attributes and qualities with particular spiritual energies. I saw that popcorn is a symbol they use to trigger the memory dealing with children, happiness, games,

117

etc., hence Npu. I flash back to the present time with a greater understanding and now it makes sense to me what spirits are and why certain offerings are requested.

In less than five minutes, I felt like I went back in time or shifted to another reality and got some insightful information that will improve my life. And, this is the reason for working with spirits because they are our like our ancient card catalogue for life!

Think about it this way. Somewhere in your mind there is a solution specifically for all of your problems. There is an answer to whatever ails you. We always hear people saying that God, the Supreme Being, the Universe, the Infinite Spirit, etc. is all–knowing, all powerful and everywhere, but how many people act on it? And, how many people really believe it? This in my opinion is proof, which means that all we have to do is be patient, go within and retrieve the internal book for what we want. The way we check out the book is by talking to our library technicians that over specific departments within us – our spirits.

God is the Infinite Intelligence, like deep space, and beneath the Divine are smaller infinite intelligences, which are like the planets in space. So the representative of the Divine Infinite Intelligence of Beauty and Love we call in Kamitic Nebhet. The representative of the Divine Infinite Intelligence of Power and Justice in Kamitic is called Hru Aakhuti. The representative of Divine Infinite Intelligence that Opens the Way to Opportunities and Removes Obstacles is called Npu and so on. All of these intelligences exists throughout the universe and exist in the deepest parts of your mind, which remember is made in the image of God.

Here's the thing. You already have these experiences so it is not like you have to go and learn something new. The

118

thing that is hindering most of us is that we have been taught to ignore these experiences and put our faith in only what we can physically see. For instance, if I had not had my little experience where I had to learn how to trust my intuition, in the previous example when I saw some ancient Africans cataloguing certain objects like popcorn with the spirit Npu. I would have ignored that vision because I have no one to authenticate and validate that what I witnessed was real. And, this is how the enemy gets us. By making us doubt and discredit our intuition.

I chose to accept that this is how my ancestors programmed their spirit because it makes sense. I now have a better understanding and I use this sacred science extensively now. To determine if it is maa (my truth); all I need to do is test it and see if it works. To determine if it is Maa (the Absolute Truth), we just need several people to do it and to continue doing, because it could be that this particular method was only used by my ancestors and those who were in the same clan. This is how we authenticate if something is real or not from our ancestral shamanic perspective. We based it upon if it works, not if it could be found in some book written by an author outside of the culture.

This as you can see is an art and science and now I know that whenever I want a particular thing or to achieve a particular goal. All I need to do is find the symbol I need to trigger the higher part of the spirit. Fortunately, all of these symbols are tied with our spirits, so by understanding the spirit. Essentially you understand the symbol needed to unlock the mysteries within your mind.

Why Working with Jesus Just Won't Cut It

One of my favorite comedies of all times is the movie *Major League*, which is about the Cleveland Indians baseball team. In the movie there is a character named Pedro Cerrano played by actor Dennis Haysbert, who supposedly defects from Cuba to the United States for religious freedom in order to practice Vodou. The funny thing about the Cerrano is that he is a power hitting outfielder that can't hit a curve ball so he enlists the aid of one of his spirits whom he calls Jobu to help him. Of course, all of this is fictional but one of the memorable scenes of the movie is that Cerrano gets into a little discussion with veteran pitcher and teammate Eddie Harris played by Chelcie Ross, who tells Cerrano that he might "consider accepting Jesus Christ as his lord and savior." Cerrano's response to Harris (and I am paraphrasing) is that "Jesus Christ is good. I like him, but no good for curve ball." This response prompted Harris to ask, "Are you telling me Jesus Christ can't hit a curve ball?"

The whole scene was hilarious because it highlighted a spiritual dilemma that exists amongst most people. You see most people don't understand the psychology of religion because they don't understand energy. Even the people that claim they understand the psychology of religion don't, because they still find themselves locked in the good versus evil paradigm. The reason is because most people practice religion out of a sense of duty and tradition. This is the main reason I am against organized religion because over time this man made system deteriorates resulting in a loss of spirituality.

Again, most of the heinous crimes committed in the history of the planet were by religious people. Religious people are easily swayed into committing atrocities because they are emotional, reactionary individuals that are totally dominated by the superficialities of their sahu. This is why like animals, they will fight, war and kill others based upon the slightest difference of an opinion as to what name to call God. Religious people only identify with our differences and similarities based upon what they can see. They never go beyond the dogma because they have a strong impression of a savior on their sahu.

If we will recall, strong impressions are made using imagery, symbols, music, etc. This means that regardless if you are an active member in a religion or not, if you close your eyes and still have an image of Jesus or some other savior. It is because there is an impression that was made upon your sahu usually involving music, dance, etc. This isn't a deep impression but a powerful one, which is the reason religious people only believe or are infatuated with God, but don't know God. This explains why so long as things are going well in a person's life (happy relationships, money in their pockets, food on the table, stead work, decent health, etc. They are happy and pleased with God, but as soon as all hell breaks loose where they lose their job, health fails, money problems, relationship problems, etc. Most people are crying, "Why God? Why me? What have I done to deserve this?" It is all because the impression is superficial. It should now make sense why so many people after hearing a lengthy sermon will right after service is out, lose their holy ghost and cuss out or harm another. Again, the teachings of the savior only addressed the fruit. It didn't penetrate the superconscious grounds of the ba.

When Cerrano said, "Jesus is good but not good for curve ball." I am not sure if the writers intended this but the message I got, which explains the reason so many people continue to work with angels, saints, spirits, etc. is that the iconic image and message of Jesus is that you can "do

121

whatever you want and I (Jesus/God) will save you." A lot of times however, we don't need to be saved. We just need to take responsibility for our actions and find a way to do things our self, which is how in the end of the movie Cerrano overcomes the dreaded curveball.

Spirituality is about taking responsibility for your development of your spirit and it is very difficult to do this when you have the image of Jesus (or some other savior) in some passive conquered posture impressed upon your mind. Some people think that the ethnicity of the savior has some bearing but it doesn't because remember our sahu (the lower spirit or subconscious) doesn't discriminate between good and bad, right and wrong, black or white. It lacks conscious reasoning. The image of the savior however makes a strong impression and conveys a message to be loving and trusting in God. It doesn't however, instill in people to take responsibility for their own salvation, so that they can improve their life.

In other words, Jesus (and the images of other saviors) are only concerned with the afterlife. For anything else, the image of Jesus didn't provide any concrete guidelines for the subconscious; hence Jesus is not good for the curveballs in life.

Think about it. You are a woman having problems with your husband and you pray to Jesus. The image of Jesus comes to mind, but Jesus had no wife (at least that church

122

body would officially acknowledge), he didn't even deal with women a lot, so what is the message that is received from Jesus? What is the end result image to focus upon? The lack of a concrete image would force the sahu of most to arrive at a conclusion based upon an individual's personal experience. Have you ever heard some women say, "Jesus is my husband" or something to the effect? This is the reason why. It would be more advantageous for a woman having marital issues to pray to Joseph and Mary then it would be to Jesus, because it provides a concrete instructional image for the sahu.

This is the reason for working with various archetype spirits because their stories cover the entire human experience. For instance, if the same woman were to work with the archetype spirit for love like Nebhet, Hetheru, Oshun, Mama Chola, Venus, Aphrodite, even Mary Magdalene and programmed that image into her sahu (subconscious self). She may get a message intuitively after reading their stories to be sweeter and less combative, more seducing, etc. because these are all Venusian energies that have inspired and halted wars, or. That she is being too weak minded, docile, gullible, and she doesn't respect or finf beauty in herself. There is no way Jesus could have told her this, but now she sees what she has to do in order to improve her relationship.

It is the same for fighting an enemy. People can say what they want to say, but there are people in this world that don't want you to succeed. And, you didn't even have to do anything to them. Just the fact that you seem happy or said hello, these people will be ready to jump you and cause serious harm to you and your loved ones. Yeah, the spirit of God may be in them but they ain't using or relying upon it. So, these individuals are called enemies and we have to recognize that and stop buying into this pseudo – spirituality.

123

When it comes to dealing with these beast men and women who are totally controlled by their emotions, ego or Set and the aapepu. The last image I need sown into my spirit (ba – sahu) is how I need to love my enemies in order to go to heaven. No! I don't think so. I need the image of a fighter, a warrior, etc. I need to sow into my ba – sahu the image that I will be protected from all forms of harm and a silly ball of white light ain't going to do it either. I need Hru Aakhuti, Ogun, Zarabanda, Archangel Michael, Saint George, etc. which would help me feel protected and safe from harm. I need a physical image that will sow the idea of me being victorious over such individuals.

As you can see, the reason for working with spirits, angels, gods, goddesses, and other nonhuman characters is because it is easier to envision them performing a specific operation than it is to focus on an abstract character focused on saving you from your sin. When you work with your spirits you reduce the amount of time illness, poverty, depression and other negative thoughts can reside in your consciousness by impressing upon your mind positive cosmic archetypes.

How the Spirits Interact With Us

Understand, we all have memories of sacred sciences within us because the sahu remember is the intelligence responsible for maintaining our physical body consciousness – including memories on a genetic level. So even if you can't consciously recall a particular memory. The sahu remembers and there is an ancestor that remembers, which is why it is important that our ba works with our sahu. The sahu you will recall will cause accidents, sabotage conscious efforts, etc. because it is reactive and is responding to certain stimuli. When we evaluate certain actions and behaviors from a higher perspective we find see that there could be a spiritual

124

explanation behind it. For instance, have you ever dropped food off your fork onto the floor or been drinking a glass of water and suddenly the glass misses your lip and spills? From an esoteric perspective these could be signs that your ancestors are hungry or thirsty, because they just like your living relatives will take your drink or food from off your plate. It is believed the dead relatives will do the same. Not only are your ancestors notorious for taking food and drink, Npu (and his spirits) are fond of rearranging and misplacing objects. Some spirits like to roam, meaning you will get a hunch out of nowhere or see them out the corner of your eye. Other times they will encourage you to move things from one place to another.

None of these events should be interpreted as a malicious event. It is just the spirits way of getting our attention and proof that the spirits don't communicate to us using metu neter (medu neter or some other archaic and symbolic language) that we aren't familiar with. They meet us where we are at and interact with us to direct our attention and help us to achieve certain goals. That being said if you don't know anything about medicine, don't expect the spirit of a doctor to come to you and teach you medicine. Any spirit that does this is most likely an imposter aapepu. Again, the spirits will meet you at whatever level you are on. The spirit of a deceased doctor will only feel comfortable communicating medical insight with another or similar colleague.

The Purpose of Science

Spirits remember are conscious, willful, sentient (emotional) energies that communicate to our ba intuitively. This means that the ba gets all of its wisdom and intuitive ideas that we receive from the deceased ab – souls of people that once walked the earth. Jung discovered this while investigating and researching his various theories, as he delved into alchemy, Eastern mysticism, Gnosticism, Mithraism and possibly Spiritism, which was very popular during his time. Today Jung is the most celebrated and quoted psychoanalyst ever because he provided a scientific way of understanding mystical experiences and occult phenomena. It was through his scholastic works it was realized that human beings are not dragged, shameful and sinful creatures that need to be saved spiritually, but are spiritual beings having a physical experience. In other words, all of our problems are due to our disconnection from our ba – spirit, which means the only way to save ourselves is to reconnect back to our omnipotent, omniscient and omnipresent ba – spirit.

It is important to understand that when we look at events but have lost the philosophy, theory and/or theology behind why it occurs, it degenerates into a superstition. Jung on the other hand provided a way to rid ourselves of superstition through his theory. This was truly a new and radical idea far different from his colleague Sigmund Freud, and when we understand the nature of the human mind. We can clearly see it was from Jung's ba. Jung discovered these radical new theories about the collective unconsciousness, archetypes, active imagination and other techniques used today, by working with his spirit guide he called Philemon.

What this means is that we all have a host of spirits that exist amongst us. We bump elbows and shoulders with them all the time. They walk in and out of our homes. We run into them on our job, at the store, etc. because all spirits are non-physical expressions of the divine. They are basically the inspirational and thoughtful influence behind everything we do.

The Relationship between the Living & Spirits

It is important to understand that spirits are on the same level as us and not above us because there are a lot of traditions that believe in the latter. As a result, they are under the impression that they have no say so in their lives and that it is the will of the spirits. These traditions believe that the spirits can roam freely and do whatever they want to human beings because human beings are vulnerable feeble minded creatures. So the spirits can possess them and make them act a fool. It is not for me to say if this is right or wrong. To these individuals this system of beliefs aids in maintaining their social order, which is the reason we always have to look at everything from a Maa perspective. That is, does it serve its purpose in bringing balance, peace and prosperity? This is the reason; it is not for anyone outside of these traditions to comment on if it is right or wrong. It is whatever works.

I can say however say that this paradigm doesn't work for me because I have a different background and cultural experience. I was raised in a Protestant Christian country by two loving Apostolic Pentecostal parents, where it was believed that spirits exist and they manifests themselves as lying spirits, jealousy spirits, cheating spirits, etc. Spirits were viewed as being intelligent annoyance that attack the weak willed who didn't keep their mind focused on Jesus. For the longest time because the people in my church didn't talk about the science behind their beliefs and didn't discuss if spirits existed or not. I entertained that thought once upon a time if God and spirits so, I had to discover for myself if this paradigm was true. After trial and error, and learning that Jesus is the Christian equivalent of Osar. It all made sense and I learned that not all spirits were bothersome distractions. Many were benevolent but they are all attracted to us based upon what we believe. Simply put, they are a reflection of what we believe and think.

127

This is the reason we had to begin by understanding the nature of our mind, because if you believe that the devil (your lower self) or some other lower entity can possess you, then he will. Not because he can, but because you believe he can so your ba – sahu creates the situation that makes it possible.

For this reason, I advocate that the relationship between the living and spirits is supposed to be like a respectful business partnership where both parties (the living and the spirit) benefits. It is not supposed to be like the relationship between a master and his slave as describe in the old horror movies, where the living does the spirit's bidding or they will be severely punished. This is just Hollywood nonsense created because people enjoy being frightened for one. Secondly it was created because many religious organizations are able to drive their membership up through fear. This is the reason so many sermonizers dwell upon the faults and ills of society versus keeping their mind on being Christ – like. By talking about what you don't like only magnifies the problem according to Code #3 of the Maa, "Maa is Harmony & Harmony Becomes What Attention is Focused On."

And, while we're on the subject, spirits don't want your soul or your first born child. Spirits don't want your blood or want you to make some ridiculous promise where you devote your life to them for all of eternity. Since spirits do not have a physical body. They want what they lack, which is the ability to physically experience. This means they can't enjoy a physical conversation, eating food, a good drink, friendship, sexual relations, etc. Imagine your favorite dish and not being able to eat it. This is how many spirits feel, which means what spirits need the most is time and energy. Part of the reason my relationship with my spirits grew was because before I had sacred space dedicated to them, and before

128

making food offerings. I entertained them in my imagination. I would call upon certain deceased relatives and ask, "How would you do this?" and I would allow the ideas come to me.

So, what the spirits want is time and energy. Time and energy can be having a conversation with your deceased loved one at their gravesite or having a party in some spirit's honor. It can be meditating on a particular image at the same time for a week or, preparing a favorite meal that a particular spirit might enjoy, because spirits miss and they want friendship, to be remembered, good deeds and praise.

This is part of the reason most spirits will eagerly enter into a partnership with the living, so that their physical needs are somewhat met. There are only a few spirits that will try to subdue the living and trick them into giving them what they want, but this is extremely rare. Again, this is stuff that movies are made of but it is not a reality.

If you accept the theory that spirits were once people and they have feelings, then it means that spirits are like most people we meet throughout our life. The only difference being that spirits don't have a physical body but they have personalities likes and dislikes, etc. just like we do. Just like there are people you can easily get along with, there are spirits that you can easily get along with. Just like there are people whom you may have a personality conflict with, there are spirits you will have a similar conflict with as well. The best way to work with any spirit is to follow the advice given in 1 John 4:1, which states "Beloved, believe not every spirit, but try the spirits whether they are of God..."

The way to try the spirit is to first, identify who the spirit is and how they can help you. Second, acquaint yourself with the spirit's likes, dislikes, history, stories, etc.

to see if there is anything that appeals to you about them, and lastly. Clearly state to the spirit what it is that you need them for or the reason you would like them to help you.

Since spirits do not have a physical body they are not able to communicate to us verbally. They instead speak to us using symbols in our dreams, visions and hunches. (Archetypes have the ability to communicate to us using natural phenomenal such as through an animal, change of weather, etc.). To interpret these messages we simply have to understand how these symbols make us feel. If you get a hunch that the spirit is communicating with you, then most likely they are so go with it. The thing is however, you should always be a little skeptical when working with spirits. Never take what a spirit tells or informs you as the absolute truth. Always, test whatever is communicated to you out first. Again, most spirits understand the purpose behind you doing this because just like you wouldn't trust a complete stranger with a large sum of money. They don't expect you to trust them either until a rapport has been established.

The way to build a rapport with any spirit is by clearly learning all that you can about the spirit. The same way you would about a living person. You do this by reading about the spirit and observing their likes and dislikes. Most spirits will differ from individual to individual, so you will need to read as much material as possible to get a general idea of the spirit. Also because many spirits have several incarnations, you can also learn about the spirit through their incarnations, like Sokar and San Alejo.

Once this has been done, when you ask the spirit for its assistance, understand that just like human beings spirits don't work for free. Some spirits love food (with no salt or small portions from one's meal), others like alcoholic drinks, while others like money (yes, real money). To understand what the spirits' needs are we have to understand that the lack of a physical body means that the things that physically affects us doesn't affect them. Spirits can't feel pleasure or pain. They aren't plagued with illness or hunger pains. Spirits can't get diabetes from eating too much candy. They can't even speak because they don't have a mouth to do so. However, when we keep in mind that they are energies, we are reminded that they communicate to us through our dreams, signs and symbols. Although technically they do not feel hunger or thirst because they cannot nourish a physical body, they are able to partake in the essences of physical things. The essence of food, drink, etc. is enough to give them the energy that they need to further their existence in the spiritual realm.

This is why most spirits will request a few simple items like a glass of water, alcoholic beverage, white candle, flowers, etc. and these are usually the basic items to always have on hand. Once the relationship between you and your spirits grows the offerings may become more elaborate. For instance, I have heard in some traditions that if some spirits help you such as in conceiving a child. The offering that is made is that the child is named after the spirit pending there is a healthy pregnancy and normal delivery. Some spirits if they helped you with your finances want a small percentage for their financial savvy. Part of the reason I write books is because it is an offering and testimony to the spirits who assisted me in making a full recovery. Other types of elaborate offerings can be donating time to a hospital ward, charity, soup kitchen, etc. All you have to do is follow your intuition and when the offering comes to your mind, see if you can fulfill it. Another type of offering that is quite common in the Latino communities are parties for the spirits where everyone who was invited is encouraged to dress in the colors of the spirit and the food that is served is in the spirit's honor. Another very popular way amongst Latin American artists is to dedicate a song to a particular spirit. The orisha Babaluaiye the Yoruba incarnation of Sokar has numerous songs dedicated to him.

As you can see, there are numerous ways to pay the spirit for their services, but whatever you do. You never make a promise to offer them something that you have no intention of getting. Whenever the spirit fulfills its end of the bargain be sure to pay the spirit for the services rendered. Understand, because spirits don't have a physical body, they have the ability to see what we cannot see and go places instantly where we cannot go, which makes them great allies on the other side. You certainly don't want to mess that up by reneging on a payment.

The Spirits of Kamta

There are all types of spirits that exist but the only individual in the Western hemisphere to document and categorize the various types of spirits was the French educator Hippolyte Léon Denizard Rivail also known as Allan Kardec. According to Kardec spirits are arranged in a type of hierarchical order sort of like a rigid class system. Kardec believed that there were three orders of spirits. The first order was called Pure Spirits and they were the highest of any type of spirits. This order was followed by an order of Good Spirits, which were composed of high, wise, benevolent and learned spirits. The final order was Imperfect Spirits, which consisted of boisterous spirits, neutral spirits, frivolous spirits and finally impure spirits.

My experience in Kamta has led me to see this spiritual arrangement differently, because when the African spirits came to North America to be with their children. Although they were from various ethnic groups and tribes, a significant

132

number of them were Fons, Wolofs and from the Kongo-Angolan region. When these spirits arrived in North America, they weren't able to hide themselves under the Catholic guise as those had done in the Caribbean and South America. Many of them instead chose to merge with the various biblical characters in the Protestant Christian tradition, like Moses, King Solomon, etc. in order to preserve and protect their memory. Many of them with this new guise survived and can be found in various folk paths, but most of them became dormant.

Centuries later when various Afro Caribbean and later African traditions came to the United States during the 1960s and 1970s Cultural Movement. Many of these spirits who had been sleep began to awaken because of the familiarity they had long ago but, when the Kamitic tradition began to take root. A number of these spirits became active because they found a working medium that they could use to catapult themselves back into our realm. Thanks to Ra Un Nefer Amen, the celebrated author of the *Metu Neter* series and founder of the Ausar Auset Society, a renaissance in ancient African traditions was created. It is because of the Ausar Auset Society, I like many others, was forever changed as we invited the Kamitic spirits into our homes, but as I stated before. My spirits changed because of the various influences I had encountered along with my near death and lupus experience. These circumstances led to the evolution of Kamta.

Since Kamta is a Kamitic shamanic tradition, the Kamitic along with the African and various Afro–Caribbean influences led me to see these spirits with lighter and heavier ab – souls who still need spiritual progress. Many of my spirits as I stated earlier were from the Kongo Angolan traditions, and they were called bakulu (ancestral spirits), basimbi (benevolent spirits similar to martyrs and saints)

133

and bankuyu (malevolent spirits similar to devils and imps). They survived in Kamta as: aakhu (ancestral spirits and guides), netcharu (guardian spirits) and aapepu (confused and misguided spirits).

Initially the spirits I encountered were syncretized with the Yoruba orishas and were interested in spiritual enlightenment. After I met Papa my spirits changed (or rather our understanding evolved) because, Papa helped me to see that we do not live in ancient Kamit where we have a kingdom and are trying to ward off foreign invaders. We do not live in a time where we are respected solely based upon our character. These are hostile times we live in as it is said in Ephesians 6:12 "...*we wrestle not against flesh and blood, but against principalities, against powers, against the rulers of the darkness of this world, against spiritual wickedness in high places.*"

Simply put, this ain't Kamit! This is a different time where there are a host of influences that we must battle on an everyday basis. Racism is real and it permeates every aspect of our life. So my spirits had to reflect this period I was in and they had to be willing to help me fight. The Kamitic spirits in their original guise were too passive, so they merged with other spirits and became aggressive – passive.

All of the spirits of Kamta are considered to be warriors in their own right, which is why they all have several incarnations. They are warriors that fight for our mind – spirit, which doesn't mean that they all have masculine aggressive energy. It simply indicates that my spirits are fighters. For instance, since, it is not enough to say and believe you are going to do right. You need to fix in your mind a concrete image of what you want. With Sokar as my guard, it is difficult for any illness to impress itself upon my

134

mind because Sokar's incarnation as San Lazaro (Saint Lazarus) helps me to obtain and maintain my health.

Please note: It is important to keep in mind that the aakhu, netcharu and aapepu are all parts of our superconscious mind that have simply been anthropomorphized.

1. Aakhu – are in general, the spirits associated with our ancestors. They are called our ancestors and spirit guides. They are our ancestral memories and can help us with spiritual perfection, protection and matters regarding our family. The aakhu are extremely ethical and moral spirits. They are responsible for building our culture and instilling cultural pride. There are several types of aakhu and they are:

    a. Biological Aakhu which are ancestral spirits related to by blood.

    b. Historical Aakhu are those ancestral spirits that are often celebrated and remembered during Black History Month, Black Awareness Day, and so on. These are ancestors that have made historic contributions and upon hearing their stories, continue to inspire people throughout the ages like Zumbi of Palmares, Nat Turner, Jacques Desalines, Harriet Tubman, Fredrick Douglas, Malcolm X, and Martin L. King Jr., etc. Most of these aakhu have biographies, documentaries, streets, buildings, statues, etc. that were named in their honor for their contribution.

    c. Cultural Aakhu are spirits that became folk heroes and heroines like John Henry, Brer Rabbit, John the Conqueror, etc. who is one of the most popular cultural aakhu throughout the Afro-diaspora.

135

Cultural aakhu are unique because they have transcended geographical boundaries and can be found in other countries usually either under the same or similar name. In order to work with these aakhu you have to be very familiar with the culture the aakhu descends from. For instance, if you don't know anything about Buddha or Kwan Yin, it would be very difficult for you to establish a rapport with these aakhu. One of the most popular cultural aakhu throughout the Afro-diaspora is that of the elder black man and woman called Uncle and Auntie:

i   Uncle and Auntie are two of the most iconic figures in the Afro – diaspora are the depiction of elder black man and woman. They have been called Francisco and Francisca in the Afro – Cuba traditions, Los Pretos Velhos (Older Blacks) in the Afro – Brazilian traditions, and Los Negros in Mexican Curanderismo traditions. Sometimes in the Cuban and Puerto Rican traditions the male is referred to as El Kongo (the Congo) and the woman is identified with La Madama or Aunt Jemina. African Americans referred to the man as Old Black Joe or Uncle and the female was commonly called Mammy, Mamma or Auntie. Now, many people have a hard time accepting these images because these iconic images were used in the United States to justify slavery and ridicule all forms of Afro – American culture, but they represented a type of generational archetype. Figuratively they are seen as the first Africans that were brought to the Americas who managed to survive to an advance age. They are considered to be the cultural links or great ancestors that ties one back to Africa, particularly the Kongo – Angolan region. It is because of these African archetypes that out of respect older black men were often called Uncle (i.e. Uncle Remus, etc.) and the older black women were called Mamma or Auntie, a practice that continues to this day even amongst non-blacks.

Figure 9: Uncle and Auntie Aakhu Overlooking the Ancestors

While American media has tried to pervert these iconic figures' stories through various mediums like Uncle Tom, Uncle Ben, Aunt Jemina, etc. The truth is that these beloved characters symbolize real people in the early African American community and Afro-Diaspora. They were very cunning and wise former slaves who passed along their ancient wisdom in a number of ways. A lot of times we honor those ancestors who physically fought against oppression but forget about those who fought against mental slavery. Uncle and Auntie remind us of their contributions.

137

Uncles (Ole Black Joe or Papas) are usually depicted as an elderly black man with white hair smoking a corncob pipe. He usually wears some type of straw hat to protect him from the scorching sun. He was called upon for his knowledge of herbs, hunting expertise and problem solving skills He was a storyteller who like most griots expressed their wisdom in fable and proverbs, such as in the Uncle Remus stories. Contrary to popular belief, most Uncles were not like Harriet Beecher Stowe's fictional Uncle Tom. True Uncle spirits were like second fathers. They would teach you lessons that your father wouldn't a lot of times to help you grow up. When you make the connection with this spirit he will inform you if he wants to be called Uncle or Poppa.

Auntie spirits were called upon for help with playing card, bone and tea leaf divination, herbal knowledge, midwife issues; help with children, and magical expertise. Like Uncle spirits Aunties in the African American community were like second Mothers. They were protective of their own especially of children. When you make the connection with this spirit she will inform you if she wants to be called Momma, Auntie or even La Madama.

d. Native American Aakhu are Native American spirits who assisted early African Americans during slavery. There are many Native American spirits that exist. The most famous is named Black Hawk but there are many others including White Hawk, Red Cloud and Thunder Dog. Their names typically give an idea to their purpose and how to work with them. Most Native American spirits I have come across are not fond of alcohol (most not all) but, they all really enjoy tobacco. In fact, it is said that the extensive use of cigars in most Afro – Diaspora practices is due to Native American introducing the herb to Africans. Native Americans aakhu are also very proud and moral spirits that have a strong affinity with nature. Many are also very strong willed, which means they will only introduce themselves to you, when they feel like. They aren't the typical pseudo environmentalists. They truly want you to have a respect for living things. For instance, in order to get the most benefit from the tobacco spirit as they have, you can't abuse tobacco.

While we're on the subject let me tell you about my experience with Black Hawk. For years, I had a Native American statue and had wanted to honor Black Hawk using it, but I couldn't connect with him. I read his history. I read how the famous Spiritist Mother Leafy Anderson first introduced Black Hawk, but still there was no connection, so I basically let the statue sit and gaze out of my front window. Now, for years, this is all that this Native American statue would do. Then one day out of the blue, while cleaning my ancestor altar Black Hawk showed himself. He revealed to me that he wanted to protect my spiritual tradition. Instantly I was reminded of the relationship that many Native Americans and African Americans shared in the past, and how they would act as lookouts for runaways. Black Hawk revealed to me that although times have changed, we live in a similar time where I could be persecuted for working with the spirits. So, he decided after all of these years to offer his service because somehow he remembered how he was treated.

This has helped to see that Native American spirits are very observant, cautious and patient. They will wait and study everything about you before deciding to work with you.

e. Teaching Aakhu are ancestral spirits that act specifically as guides. These spirits can come from another family, ethnic group, culture, etc. because they are solely interested in advancing a chosen discipline or profession. So, their sole purpose is to help others in accomplishing certain tasks. Most teaching aakhus are have an uncanny way of interceding in an individual's life. A lot of times, when a teaching aakhu is guiding an individual, the person is not even aware until they have had several "Aha" moments. For instance, think about how many people have been influenced by Albert Einstein and how many people he has helped. There are posters, t-shirts and other types of paraphernalia of Einstein all over, which continues to increase Einstein's awareness and spiritual influence. By beginning to speak to him, one can easily tap into his surviving intelligence. Teaching aakhus are unique because they are usually looked upon as being academic and skill role models. In fact, all of Napoleon Hill's *Invisible Counselors* could best be described as being teaching aakhu.

f. Mystical Aakhu are ancestral spirits that consist of biblical characters such as Abraham, Queen Esther and King David. Mystical aakhu are basically role models or what is commonly called archetypes and as previously mentioned, most of the mystical aakhu were spirits brought from Africa who merged with biblical characters in order to preserve their identity and memory. Usually mystical aakhu inspire movements to change a particular time of thinking or an Age. To get an idea how mystical aakhu work, think about Fredrick Douglas and Harriet Tubman changed how people viewed descendants of Africa and former slaves, who were both inspired by Moses. Another heroic individual whom Moses inspired was Dr. Martin L. King Jr., who commonly used similar references as Moses did such as referring to freedom as the Promise Land.

The thing that most mystical aakhu have in common is that their true story is always obscure, where it is not known if they physically existed or not like Jesus. Usually when an aakhu transcends to this point they eventually become one with a netcharu. In fact, most mystical aakhu are actually thought to be avatars or emissaries of a particular netcharu. This is why it is a common practice especially amongst Kongo influenced traditions to honor a particular spirit through the image of a Christian saint based upon their iconography instead of their history. Moses for instance is seen as being an avatar or path the netchar Djahuti based upon his identification with snakes and Djahuti's caduceus and association with the law. Saint Patrick is another example. He is invoked based upon his iconography for driving out poisons or chasing away one's enemies instead of being revered as the patron of Ireland.

Another interesting thing about mystical aakhu is that usually they are multifaceted. Take for instance, the Christian savior Jesus who for years was believed to have died for the sins of humankind because he was said to be the son of God. Now, in recent years because of the Gnostic Gospels, the world finally gets a different perspective of Jesus. Through the Gnostic texts it is learned that Jesus preached that we are divine beings experiencing a physical existence and not sinned at all. This revelation has inspired a new movement amongst many devotees, which is a prime example of how mystical aakhu function.

Please keep in mind this is general information about the spirits. Don't expect everyone's spirits to be exactly the same. For instance, I my Auntie is honored next my Uncle spirit, but I remember seeing Papa's Auntie or La Madama venerated next to his Ellegua (the Yoruba Npu). In fact, I remembered him telling me that his La Madama was married to his Ellegua. Was he right or wrong? According to his *la manera (his way)* he was correct and that is how this particular spirit worked to manifest the things he wanted in his life, and guess what? That's all that matters...the physical end results. So, it didn't matter what anyone believed and I am telling you the same thing. It doesn't matter what anyone thinks, so long as you are not physically harming another to get results. You have the right to do whatsoever you want.

2. Netcharu (neteru, netjeru) are the pure and benevolent guardian spirits of Kamit. To understand the nature of the netcharu it has to be understood that the Kamitic people did not have a pan-religion where everyone worships some idol. In fact, they didn't have a religion per se where one attends a temple to

142

worship a Supreme Deity on a regular basis. Western archeologists refer to the spiritual practices of non-Western people as a religion because they have no other means of defining it. Once this is accepted it will be clear that there were various ethnic groups or tribes that existed in Kamit with their own unique cultural identity. Based upon my research and personal experience, the original netcharu were the leaders or figure heads of the nine tribes that inhabited, maintained and composed of what we know today as Ancient Kamit. (Originally there were ten but Set was ousted, resulting in nine. More about Set later). The actual Kamitic tribal names may have been lost but the identity and cultural influence of the clan was preserved in the characterization of the netcharu. I believe these nine tribes came together in order to survive and overcome a common threat. Initially this threat was foreign influence but later it was expanded to include Set and his 72 conspirators.

So what we call the netcharu (netjeru, neters, etc.) I believe is really a spiritual collective or a group of spirits that shared and continue to share a common cultural bond, who have organized under the tutelage of a particular netchar. In other words, they are spiritual tribes consisting of a number of hundreds of spirits. This is important to understand because as with people, when a spirit is called upon unexpectedly, he or she may not be home. However, other minor spirits of the same tribe or similar incarnation has been appointed to be the netchar's helpers, will usually take it upon themselves to answer the request that was sent forth. This is the only way a single spirit is able to respond to the numerous requests sent to them single handedly. For instance, Npu may be called upon to open the way, but can be represented using his

Catholic incarnation as El Niño de Atocha or someone else may see him as the Apostle Peter, whereas another may choose to represent him as the Hindu divinity Ganesha, and so on. When these different incarnations manifest themselves to you, they are the netchar revealing how its energy will manifests itself in your life. The netcharu are ancient ancestral memories associated with natural forces in the universe and within our being that have been anthropomorphized. The nine netchar are:

a. Osar – are concerned specifically with inner peace, wisdom, spiritual enlightenment and prosperity for all. Osar has no sacred numbers. His color is white the color of purity, cleanliness, knowledge, wisdom and coolness. Osar's incarnations are of course Jesus, Saint Lucy, Our Lady of Mercy, Guardian Angel, Jehovah Shalom (The Lord is Our Peace) and any archetype of peace, prosperity and wisdom or simply spiritual enlightenment. General statement of intent: "Thank you for peace, purity and wisdom."

b. Oset (Infinite Intelligence of Transformation) – is the patroness of women, mothers, single mothers and fisherman. She is the symbol of devotion especially mothers, single mothers and all who despite the overwhelming dangers and threat to her own life, continue to do what is necessary in order for children and families to be nurtured. Oset's defiance against Set makes her a revolutionary and the mother of all who desire change. Her colors are blue and white. Her number is seven. Her incarnations are the Virgin Mary, Our Lady of Miraculous Medals, are Jehovah Shammah (The Lord is There) or any protective

144

motherly archetype. Oset is called upon for
protecting and healing mothers and all children.
General statement of intent: "Thank you for love,
devotion and the protection of my family."

c. Djahuti (Infinite Intelligence of Wisdom) –are His
colors are indigo and white. His number is eight.
Since Moses was one of the few to have seen
Jehovah he is often considered to be an incarnation
of Djahuti as well as Solomon, Jehovah Ezer (The
Lord is Our Helper/Problem Solver) and any
archetype that shows an impeccable amount of
wisdom. Djahuti is called upon to help in solving all
problems. General statement of intent: "Thank you
for wisdom and the insight to solve problems
efficiently."

d. Hru (Infinite Intelligence of Authority & Power) –
are full of power and passion, and concern
themselves with helping one overcome their
(spiritual or physical) enemies. His colors are red
and white. His sacred number is six. Hru's
incarnations are King David, the Prophet Isaiah,
Saint Barbara, Jehovah Sabaoth (the Lord is Our
Commander). Hru is called upon for help in
overcome one's foes and being successful or
victorious in all areas of life. General statement of
intent: "Thank you for power, strength and victory
over my enemies."

e. Nebhet (Infinite Intelligence of Beauty & Love) – is
dedicated to helping one find peace, joy, and love.
Her colors are yellow or gold, green, pink and
sometimes even red. Her special number is the
number five. Nebhet's incarnations are Saint
Martha the Dominator, Mary Magdalene

145

(incorrectly believed to be a whore), Queen Esther, Jehovah Nissi (The Lord is Our Banner of Love) and other archetypes that use beauty, love and happiness to inspire humanity to reach greatness. Nebhet is called upon for help in obtaining and maintaining happiness. General statement of intent: "Thank you for peace, love and happiness."

f. Hru Aakhuti (Infinite Intelligence of Power & Justice) – are a group of warrior and soldier spirits that focus on all forms of protection, defense and hard work. His colors are blood or dark red. His numbers are three and four. Hru Aakhuti's incarnations are Saint George, the Prophet Elijah, the archangel Michael, and Jehovah Jireh (The Lord is Our Provider) and other archetypes that fight against the wicked and fight for justice. Some might associate him with Peter since the biblical archetype was known to carry two swords. He is called upon for help in protection from all forms of danger. General statement of intent: "Thank you for protecting me from danger seen and unseen."

g. Maat– are a set of spirits that are interested establishing and maintaining order. These spirits can be found in courtrooms and jails. Maat is the archetype of police, judges and anyone with the power to distribute justice and mercy. Her colors are sky or powder blue and yellow. Her number is two and four. Maat's incarnations are the Prophet Joseph, Virgin de San Juan, Jehovah Zidkenu (The Lord is Our Righteousness) and other archetypes that inspire faith, optimism and law. Maat is called upon for help in obtaining and maintaining order in one's life. General statement of intent: "Thank you

146

for bringing divine balance, divine order and divine truth into my life."

h. Npu (Infinite Intelligence of Opens the Way to Opportunities and Removes Obstacles) – are the most famous spirits from Kamit. They always sit near entrances and they have childlike personalities with a peculiar humor. Npus govern all roads and are the masters of all keys. They have a talent in finding anything, even things that you don't want to be found because they are curious in nature. Notice how children find their way into anything. Npu's colors are red, black and white and sometimes yellow. His number is 3, 9 and 21. His totem animals are dogs (especially feral dogs), jackals, wolves, coyotes, and crocodiles (alligators). Sometimes rodents like mice and rabbits. Npu's incarnations are El Niño de Atocha, Joseph the Dreamer, Jehovah Rohi (The Lord is Our Shepherd) for this reason Npu is often associated with the biblical Moses. Some might find it easier to associate him with the biblical Peter who is said to hold the keys of heaven (KAMTA). Npu quite simply is called upon to find better opportunities, general health and luck. General statement of intent: "Thank you for open the way and clearing obstacles in my path."

i. Sokar– assists in all forms of healing. They are resilient spirits with strong determinations that have mastered the secret of rebirth. Since many of them have faced death in their fight to overcome an illness. They have no fear of death and teach only the strong how to overcome any obstacle through persistence. Sokars can be found in all of the cemeteries taking the pain of loss and sorrow, and

147

transforming it to happiness and victory. Sokars are the patron spirits of beggars, hermits, and misers. All of Sokar spirits have in renewal, hard work, healing and struggle in common. His colors are white, indigo and yellow. His number is 13. Because Sokar can easily lose interest in the beauty of the world, he is sometimes offered rum, honey and cologne or perfume to remind Sokar of the beauty of life. For this reason Sokar's incarnations are Saint Lazarus (San Lazaro), Saint Alexius (Alejo), the biblical Job, Saint Jude, Jehovah Rapha (The Lord is our Healer) and any archetype who succeeds after overcoming extreme hardships. Sokar is called upon for obtaining and maintaining perfect health. General statement of intent: "Thank you for obtaining and maintaining perfect health."

j. Bastet – is not one of the original nine but she is a very prominent spirit that walks with Sokar and Hru. Living in the Midwest where there is a lot of wind gust, gave me an opportunity to meet her and understand why she wears a lioness mask. Lately, there have been a lot of tornadoes and other deadly storms. Since, storms fall under Set's ruler ship, thunderstorms metaphorically speaking is a fight between Hru and Set. Bastet is the roaring wind that accompanies Hru's ground shaking thunder. Her colors are multicolor. Bastet creates quick change and is thanked for bringing fast results.

Repeating the general statement of intent over a period of time is enough to build a strong rapport with the netcharu. You will know that a connection has been established when all of sudden you intuitively begin receiving messages and hunches. The message from the spirit doesn't have be dramatic but you will know what it is when it occurs. As was mentioned above regarding the aakhu, the same applies in regards to the netcharu, which is don't expect each of the netcharu to be the same. We each have an Osar, Oset and Npu spirit and so on, but each spirit is unique in its own little way. So, don't expect everyone's netcharu to act and behave in the same manner. For instance, my Npu may like a particular brand of cigar whereas another may prefer to smoke a tobacco pipe.

3. Set and the Aapepu – the aapepu are confused and misguided spirits commonly referred to as ghosts. Since everything in nature has its opposite, just like there is a collective of benevolent spirits, there is one for negative spirits. These are the ab – souls of individuals who for whatever reason didn't fulfill their purpose. Most of these spirits were not evil individuals in life just confused, and "As above, so below" in death they continue to be confuse, which makes them dangerous.

The lord of the Aapepu is Set also known as Baphomet. Contrary to popular belief, Set is not the epitome of evil. He simply symbolizes an arrogant, chaotic, rash and emotional state of being. He also represents old, outdated and negative collective ancestral memories that exist in our mind and throughout the Universe, which is why he is considered the lord of the aapepu.

Set is the lord of all forms of chaos. He therefore can be petitioned to prevent arguments, fights, and mischiefs, etc.

This means that when we engage in chaotic and destructive behavior, we are is essence creating a pathway for the aapepu to manifest themselves in our life.

Building a Rapport with Your Spirits

Assuming your house is cleansed of physical debris. Due to limited resources and time, I will discuss very briefly how to build a het aakhu (spirit house), which is basically a shrine for all of the spirits. I would like to spend more time on erecting a het netcharu (a guardian spirits house) for the spirits and how to work with it. So, let's begin.

I have mentioned this before and I have no problem giving credit where credit is due, but part of the inspiration for this shrine comes from the Espiritismo Cruzado tradition (Afro – Cuban Cross Spiritism). I learned it from my Papa who encouraged me to adapt and modify it so that it addressed my needs, and this is how this particular shrine came about.

Now that credits and accolades have been administered, if you have been following the evolution of the Maa Aankh, I am sure you realized by now that the shrine is a reflection of your inner mind – particularly your superconscious mind. The basic shrine also called the first floor of the het is dedicated to the aakhu. This is where you would place photos of your deceased loved ones, icons of cultural aakhu, etc. Even the last objects that a particular aakhu used prior to death can be placed on here, because the purpose is to tap into their knowledge so you can improve your life.

Place nine clear glasses in the center and fill with fresh water. (Some people claim it is best to use spring water, etc. I have found ordinary tap water works just fine.) Behind the main glass should be an ankh or crucifix with your Papa or Uncle spirit to the left and Momma or Auntie spirit to the right. A border made of seashells should be used to enclose the altar and this is the basic set up. In addition, you can place flowers on your altar but remember that as soon as the petals began to fall you must clean them up (anything that reflects death attracts negative energies). I personally think it is too much of a hassle trying to pick up petals that may fall into glasses.

This is why I personally prefer to burn incense like Frankincense, or sandalwood for my aakhu instead. I include a small cup of fragrances like Florida Water and my favorite cologne. If you have no problem doing this then, offer you r aakhu white mums. Yellow mums are also a good choice. I also offer my aakhu strong black coffee, cigars, a white candle and any other special request I get a hunch for like spearmint chewing gum, which my grandmother loved. Again, follow your intuition. Obvious **DO NOT BURN CANDLES NEAR FLAMMABLE OBJECTS**.

The second story is dedicated to the netcharu. It consists of specialized hets for a particular netcharu. For instance, in the center of the photograph below is a Chango Macho representing my Hru and to his side is Santa Barbara acting as his sister or bride. Hru is sitting inside of a clay pot filled with herbs, soils and all types of things needed to make the connection to Hru. To the far right is a Nebhet pot with an image of Saint Martha the Dominator and a toy snake resting at her feet, because these are all icons that deal with love. Sometimes Nebhet has to be tough. There are also things pertaining specifically to this spirit inside her pot. Behind Nebhet is Bes, the little dwarf like spirit. In front of Nebhet is Oset.

You can place other items on the het to energize them with your personal energy as well. For instance, my herst (sacred necklaces) are being worn by my Hru. There are also gems, crystals, stones and charms on the het, not to mention

151

Florida Water, rum, sweet jars (for sweetening individuals), etc. used specifically for spiritual purpose. Again, the het is KAMTA.

Figure 10: Two Story Spiritual House (Het)

As you can see, there are Kamitic, African and European icons on this sacred space dedicated to the netcharu because I said, they are all seen as incarnations of the same netchar. For instance, my Sokar is represented by both Saint Lazarus and Saint Alex or San Alejo because both deal with resurrection and rebirth from a different perspective. St. Lazarus is more like a physical rebirth, whereas San Alejo is more like an intellectual rebirth. As you can see, the two story het makes a strong impression of the spirit realm in KAMTA.

Another thing, I mentioned this before but it must be kept in mind that syncretism doesn't occur intellectually but spiritually. Our mind –spirit does not make a distinction between race and ethnicity, but our intellect however does. If you intellectually place a St. Barbara statue upon your altar then it will appear in your mind's eye that you have a defiant white saint, because you are approaching the subject from a TASETT perspective (Beta trance). You are seeing the issue from a superficial perspective. When you approach it from a KAMTA perspective St. Barbara appears to be part of Hru's clan. Some might even go as far as to say, a spiritual sister, or even one of his brides, because KAMTA allows magical thinking. St. Martha the Dominator could be seen as one of Nebhet's sisters or even her daughter. Again, the purpose of magical thinking is not to convince others of it, but your own lower, subconscious self in order to create miracles in your life.

Creating a Het Netchar (Guardian Spirit House)

The het netchar is a house for a specific netchar and the spirits associated with him or her. It is built on the basis that spirits respond best to the idea of "like attracts like". The het acts as a psycho – spiritual support system that intensifies the faith in yourself. This means it is very important that the objects or symbols you choose resemble the character and energy of your spirit, and its purpose, because the items placed in the het strengthens the psychic link between you, the spirits and the purpose of the het.

Since everyone will eventually want to have a het for Npu, the messenger spirit that opens the doors to opportunities and protects us all by closing doors on those roads that would lead us down the wrong path. Npu's het may contain soils from crossroads, soil from a bank, soil from a graveyard so that he can enter into the spiritual realm and

Figure 11: Model Npu Altar (Het) based on Personal Workings

cross back over[10]; a dagger for protection, a whistle to get our attention and signal approaching danger, skeleton keys to unlock any doors, etc. A het built for Nebhet might have five fish hooks on it since figuratively speaking love interests are referred to as fish. Oset's het might have a small fishing net

---

[10] Don't forget it is always about Maa (divine balance, divine order, divine truth, divine reciprocity, etc.). Don't just take soils and things without paying for them. When taking anything from nature, always state your purpose and ask permission to do so. When you get a hunch that it is okay, leave something in return to express your gratitude like a slice of fruit, tobacco, etc. This ritual act will ensure that the energy is right.

or a toy boat, which she used to retrieve the body of Osar. You have to get into the magical thinking (Alpha to Theta) in order for this to work. Remember symbols are how the spirits communicate.

Also, when building a het for your netcharu, it must stir your emotions and feelings, in order to convince your sahu of its efficacy. If the spirit's het is unappealing looking, then it is going to be unappealing to the spirit. If the het is attractive to you, then it will be attractive to the spirit. For example, the Npu het above has a set of keys, an open lock and four skulls facing the four directions symbolizing his mastery over the spirits of the crossroads. The analogy as you can see is simple.

In the creation of my spirits' het I have found that the hardest part of this whole process is picking symbols based upon how you feel versus what you think. This is because our intellect gets in the way, but don't fret. This happens only because you are not in a KAMTA state (Alpha or Beta trance). You are anxious and nervous. When this happens, calm yourself and enter into KAMTA, then simply trust the spirits. Know that if a particular spirit wants to work with you, they will provide you with the inspiration and provision. Then one day, out of the blue, you will get the motivation to build their het. This is part of the learning process in understanding the spirit. Just have patience and go with it. To help you in this process begin by first asking your aakhu to assist you in creating a het for the particular spirit.

Second, write down a statement of what you want the spirit to do or to help you with (See the above section). You have to ask yourself, what is that you want your spirit to protect you from subconsciously. Is it illness, poverty, strife, etc.?

The objects that go into your spirit's het should be thought of as tools that the spirit uses to get the job done. Most protective netcharu for instance will all have some sort of weapon (a cutlass, knife, machete, etc.) for cutting things like obstacles and protection. To personalize these items you may be inspired to purchase it in the netchar's colors, paint the tool the netchar's colors, or even string some beads in the color of the netchar and using rubber cement decorate the tool. For instance, I found a red and black flashlight, which I purchased and offered to Npu because it was in his colors. The analogy is simple. The flashlight would be used to help him see things that are usually hidden.

Everything that you give the spirit will usually go inside (or on the side) of the spirit's het. These items once offered to the spirit becomes energized with their energy, as it belongs to them, this includes any money that is offered to them. So, don't give them something that you may need to give or share with another spirit. Most of the spirits will request that their het be made out of a clay pottery pot or an iron pot. Do not use a plastic or a galvanized bucket, the spirit will not stay. They are very organic and want the most natural things you can get for them. Older African Americans made these houses in the past out of clay pots, jugs, wooden boxes, dolls, etc.

Since symbols (not metu neter, medu neters or hieroglyphic writing) are the language of our ba and sahu, and we all react and relate to symbols differently, meaning for instance an owl might mean wisdom to one individual but indicate death for another. I cannot tell you or even give you a list of the objects that should be placed inside the het. This is how the relationship between you and your spirit begins. To help you along the way, call upon the netcharu and ask them to help you in make a het for them to reside in. For instance, if constructing a het for Hru Aakhuti, you would be saying, "Hru Aakhuti. Help me to construct a het for you and your spirits to reside in order to protect me and keep me and my loved ones safe from seen and unseen danger." Then place items inside that will help the spirit fulfill its purpose like knives, weapons, etc. and possibly a toy, plastic or plaster skull to represents the warrior spirits. Whatever you do, **DO NOT USE A REAL SKULL**. You don't know where these skulls came from for one and what energies are attached to them. It is safer and more convenient to just use regular toy skulls that can be purchased at a hobby store or sold during Halloween. Remember, we are concerned with the symbolism. For a more natural feeling you might choose plaster skulls instead of plastic.

When all of the items have been placed inside of the het, chant the spirit's name while focusing on it. Try to do this for at least 10 to 30 minutes. Once you sense that the spirit is present, inform it as to how you will feed it, for instance by offering it water, a candle, etc. Again, follow your intuition. Baptize the het by spraying three mouthfuls of rum and three puffs of cigar smoke on it. Then offer the spirit a candle.

Every time you feed your spirit, it gets stronger. Now this is the time when silly ideas from horror movies or crazy thoughts from superstitious religious past, enter into our awareness. So, I must state again. Your spirits are not going to take over you or harm you in any way. They are your allies. They are your guides and guardians. If you wish for them to cease to exist, then stop feeding them energy and paying them any mind. They won't wither and die because they don't have a physical body remember, they are energy. They will however just fade away back into the inner depths of your mind like one voice amongst a crowd of people. This is an excellent way to think of spirits, that by building a het you are giving a voice to one out of billion.

When you give your spirits energy, it does so happen that if it acquires enough energy. It can even make itself visible to others. Meaning you will see an apparition of it out of the corner of your eye or other spirits associated with it. Again, there is no need to be alarm. This simply means that your netchar's het is growing and the netchar may soon request a larger clay or iron pot as a het. I remember when I first built a het for my Hru Aakhuti, it was a clay pot. He didn't like it because pottery breaks, so eventually I got a small iron pot. He was pleased but it grew pretty fast after putting various tools inside that he could use for defense. I ended up purchasing a larger iron pot and I felt like he was pleased.

Don't shortcut this process. You may get the inclination after looking on the internet to put the same things on your netchar's het like offering Hru Aakhuti several machetes. But again if there is no real connection. You will end up wasting a lot of money and time. If your Hru Aakhuti didn't ask for all those machetes, then don't give it to him. As I have said before, this is Kamitic shamanism and it is not about mimicking what others do. It is about living your life according to the principles of Maa based upon direct revelation from your Osar.

Once you have a real connection, it will not take much to call upon your netchar because all you have to do is see their het in your mind's eye.

It is suggested that you feed your spirits after tending to your aakhu. You have to think of your spirits as partners on the other side of the veil of life. We do not worship our spirits. We don't beg and plead for our spirits to help us either. They are not superior over you. They are like a super extension of you. They exist because you exist and vice versa so, understand that this is a partnership that you created – not them. We work with them, which means give them commands as to what we want done in a commanding tone. If you call upon a spirit and it is not successful. Remind the spirit of its purpose and charge it with its purpose and feed it, its energy. As I mentioned before, when I am looking for something, I ask Npu to help me to find it and in return I will give him a cigar. This usually works, but sometimes he requires a little bit more convincing, so I tell him in return for his help. I will offer him some rum and candy. This is how rapports work in TASETT – the physical, so it is the same in KAMTA – the spiritual.

Some of the netchar you will find might be a little difficult to work with but again, this is a reflection of the physical realm. Say for instance, you have a very hot temperament because your main guardian is Hru but you need some Oset or Nebhet work done. Both of these feminine netchars are kind of easy and slow moving. You can offer them a red candle but it still won't get them to move as fast as you want, because they are teaching you to patience. Eventually, you will come around and they will be like in exchange for their help they want molasses or honey, which are both slow flowing substances. So, you have to take this into consideration when working with them as well. They are all willing to work with you but you have to be willing to work with them as well. Again, it is all about Maa and the more you see it in the supernatural. The more you will be able to apply it to your affairs in the natural.

I hope you can see the exchange in Maa that is occurring. Understand the objects that are offered have their own spiritual energy, which means you might not understand what the spirit needs the object for until after the fact. For instance, I have offered money to my spirits knowing they can't use it physically, but it is the idea of sacrifice that

159

wanted. Once that money was placed in their het, it was never removed. Again, it is all about Maa. To help you in deciding what your spirits require in exchange, you might want to use the oracle explained earlier. For invocations, see the following lesson.

As you may have noticed, there is a lot of trial and error in this tradition, due to the fact that it is *Sin Regla (Without Rule)*. The advantage is that if you were to go to an orthodox tradition that has prepared het's made. Then you would have to learn how the individual that created the het works the spirit. In other words, you would be learning their system. This is how our aakhu in North America worked the spirit and I am re – presenting it here, so that you can rediscover your own system, your own way, your own maa.

Alternative Altars

That being said, there are a few letters and emails I received from people stating how they could not erect a full altar because of their living conditions. Again, one of the beauties of this tradition is that everything occurs within the mind, so if you are not able to erect an altar. Take an image, photo or symbol and venerate the spirit through this medium.

Taken hints from our early ancestors who drew the cosmogram on colonoware, we can draw the Maa Aankh on and underneath various objects using regular chalk, cascarilla, efun or Pemba chalk, pencil or carve it if you want something a little permanent. It can be drawn under the base of a statue or figurine, etc. In fact, this is one of the advantages of knowing the incarnations of the netcharu because you can place any statue in plain sight and no one will really question it. For instance, *Nino El Atocha* an incarnation of Npu greets visitors at my front door.

160

The Maa Aankh can also be drawn on the back of an image or picture. When this is done it becomes an opening or portal for the spirit. The image can then be placed in your billfold or purse. To feed the spirit residing in a photo, take the image and while holding your hands together – thus sandwiching the image – thank the spirit and ask it to continue to bless you, protect you, watch over, etc.

You can also draw the Maa Aankh underneath a pot. Then, for instance, place a cactus plant placed inside; it becomes a portal for Hru Aakhuti since this is the netchar that deals with sharp, metal objects. In addition you can also put other sharp objects such as razors, rusty nails, etc. inside the pot. Don't fear, just trust your intuition. To draw the Maa Aankh:

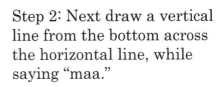

Step 1: Beginning from the left draw a horizontal line to the right, while saying "Nyun."

Step 2: Next draw a vertical line from the bottom across the horizontal line, while saying "maa."

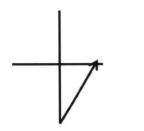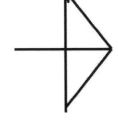

Step 3: From the bottom of

Step 4: From the right side of the horizontal arm, draw a

161

the vertical line draw a diagonal line connecting to the right of the horizontal line, while saying "Shu."

diagonal line to the top of the vertical line, while saying "Tefnut."

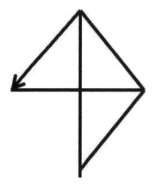

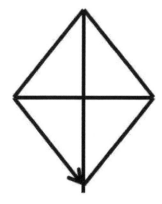

Step 5: From the top of the vertical line, draw another diagonal line but this time to the left of the horizontal line, while saying "Shu."

Step 6: From the left of the horizontal line, draw a diagonal line to the bottom of the vertical line, while ending by saying "Tefnut."

Step 7: Complete the cycle by drawing from the bottom of the diagram a counter clockwise circle connecting all of the arms. As you do this, say the following invocation, "Es Khepera, Ra, Ra Atum en Amun Ra." This is a salutation to the Almighty God, Nebertcher that simply translates as "Greetings/Hail to the One that Governs Birth, Life, Death

and Rebirth."

There are all sorts of alternatives. The idea is that wherever you draw the Maa Aankh to make a portal for the spirit, that you treat it as a sacred space. This is why it is a good idea to use chalk, because that way if you are finished, you can erase it.

Common Offerings

The thing to remember about offerings is that spirits don't work for free, no more than you do. Just like you go to work and expect at the end of a job to get a paycheck. Spirits expect the same thing, so when they finish a job. Although most of the netcharu have preferences, you can just about offer the spirit anything and they will appreciate it so long as it is offered with gratefulness, honor and respect. Always pay them when the job is done.

- Coffee – is offered to make the spirits alert.

- Water – is the common refreshment that is given to the spirits. Most spirits will accept.

- Candles – are offered to bring light, strength and security to a situation.

- Candy & Gum – these are some of the things that our aakhu miss the most. If your aakhu chewed a particular type of gum or ate a particular type of mint, offer it to them.

- Liquor – a sort of spiritual fuel. Most will accept beer and liquor except for Osar who cannot be offered any alcoholic beverages.

- Toys – toys are used to symbolize an objective and can be used to symbolize a tool. Some common toys offered are toy cars, toy trucks, toy guns, toy grenades, toy animals (snakes, rats, bugs, etc.), toy handcuffs, etc.

- Tobacco – the most common tobacco product that is used were cigars, but many of our aakhu also smoked pipe tobacco and chewed tobacco (not snuff). Cigars smoke helps to clear away negative energy and spiritual obstacles. Most spirits aakhu and netcharu will accept it. Occasionally even some of the netcharu like Hru and Oset will want a little bit of cigar smoke.

Caring for Your Hets

Generally speaking you should not allow anyone to touch your hets. Again, the hets are a reflection of your inner mind. Just like you wouldn't want anybody and everybody poking around in your mind, you shouldn't want anyone and everybody poking around on your het. If at all possible they should be kept in a separate room away from prying eyes. Some of your spirits will request that they are placed in an areas that are strictly private, but you are in control. If you can honor the request do so. If not explain your reasoning and keep going.

Where there are children involve, when they begin to show a little bit of maturity. You might want to explain to them that it is a family secret and then you may proceed to introduce it to them.

164

When it comes to a husband and wife, unless your spirits have agreed to share the space, which can be determined through divination, it's probably best that both keep separate hets. They can be placed in the closet. Note that some spirits don't appreciate this but again, if they want something better tell them to help you, so you can make better provisions. In some cases, the husband's het might be requested to be placed in the living room so that it provides security for the entire home. The wife's het might be requested to be placed in the den, hallways, kitchen, etc. where she can provide hearth and warmth to the household.

Your hets should be a thing of beauty; after all they are a reflection of the most powerful thing that the Almighty God created – your mind. When you gaze or even think about your het, it should inspire you and that's how you know it is working in your favor. It is also a tool of power so you can rest other items like your charms, divination shells, etc. on it as well.

Your glasses should be washed and refreshed on a weekly basis like on a Saturday. Some suggest Monday because it starts the work week, but I find this a little difficult to manage with getting ready to work. Now, on washing the glasses, a lot of people from the Latin American community use blessed holy water from a Catholic church, but I was taught that this was not necessary. It is whatever you are comfortable with. As I have told you before, I was raised in a Protestant country with Pentecostal parents, so emphasis on water blessed by a priest doesn't mean much to me as blessed oil does. So, the glasses can be washed with soap and water and allowed to air dry. If you burn incense use a damp sponge to wipe of ashes. Also, if you offer flowers remember to get falling petals. If you want to use a white tablecloth be sure that if it becomes filthy that you wash it.

There should be no debris around your het aakhu and het netcharu.

Remember that your hets are a reflection of your inner mind. The last thing you want is some visitor to your house asking what a particular item means, because based upon their affiliation and background, practices like burning candles appears evil. It will take too long for you to explain it to them. Just give them a copy of the books instead.

This is not a religion, so if you falter for any reason, don't beat yourself up about it. The spirits aren't going to get angry with you because you failed to offer some water, etc. Never forget that the purpose of this repetitive ritual is because through repetition of metaphors and symbols we are able to influence our sahu. The spirits are fed from the time and energy you offer them, so if you aren't able to tend to your altar because you are out of town, or whatever the case. You can do so through your imagination.

Got to Get Undignified

I hear people say that they will never talk to their spirits in a harsh manner. Well, I don't know about these individuals but the whole purpose of working with the spirits in the first place is so that you can express yourself the way you want. That means if you have to cuss to get things moving, by all means say what is in your heart. The spirits are real and they want you to be real. That is foolishness that you think you can offend God or the spirits with a harsh word. This is not ancient Greece where the god Zeus will strike down. No. These are your spirits, who have been watching over you since the beginning. I mean seriously, if you don't use Old English to speak normally, why would you use it when working with your spirits? This is what always got me about books on Egyptian prayers and hymns. Talk to your spirits like you would do a good friend. Yes, be respectful but be real at the same time.

Now that I got that off my chest I know a lot of people have problems with Christianity. Yes, there is a direct link between many of the concepts, principles and scriptures found in the bible when compared to the Kamitic texts. Yes, if you turn to Psalms 46 in the King James Bible, you will find that Shakespeare who was 46 may have covertly found a way to put the word "shake" 46 words into the psalms and "spear" 46 words from the end.

The point is who cares because the bible is a tome of power and our ancestors knew this regardless if you choose to believe it or not. We have to ask ourselves how is it that these people were able to use the bible as a tool against oppression and segregation, whereas we can't. What is it that is different today that didn't exist back then? The answer is that those people backed then believed in God and the spirits compared to what people deal with today. They used the bible as a tool because it put them in a magical mindset or Alpha, and this is what many of us have lost the ability to do. The whole purpose of the Maa Aankh is to help you to get this back, so that it doesn't matter what book you use. You can create the life that you want.

Lesson 4:
Using Rituals to Work the Superconscious Mind

The difference between meditation and ritual is that the aim of meditation is to acquire or obtain insightful information using symbols. Ritual on the other hand, focuses upon achieving observable and tangible objectives through the manipulation of symbols. A ritual is any act combined with spoken words that is performed repetitively over a period of time. There are different types of rituals, such as ceremonial rituals, such as the inauguration of a leader like the president of an organization or country, and there are and religious rituals like the reciting of Hail Mary in the Roman Catholic Church and the Islamic salat or ritual prayers. But, all rituals are created in order to do one thing and that is to build thoughtforms.

Thoughtforms are emotional energy accompanied by a thought that encourages an individual to achieve certain goals. For instance, the Pledging of Allegiance, the presidential inauguration, the singing of the Star Spangled Banner at sporting event, etc. are all rituals that were create a thoughtform encouraging patriotism for the United States. While religious rituals create thoughtforms that encourage devotion towards one's religion.

All rituals when initially perform; create a temporary emotional change in the individual undergoing the ritual intellectually. This is because if you will recall, our ab – soul or conscious has difficulty remembering or recalling memories but it can rationalize. It however, relies upon the sahu – subconscious self, which has faulty reasoning skills but an excellent memory. A ritual therefore, combines symbols and rational ideas, which a strong impression upon the sahu and ba. This is the reason people will remember a wedding ceremony, a baptism, etc. because for small amount of time, it stays on the individual's mind. In other words, they are constantly reflecting on it and the whole ritual stays in their awareness.

People who sincerely believe in baptism will feel as if they are "born again" because the ritual truly signified to them that they were washed of all of their "sins" and other wrongdoings. If more people truly understood the significance of marriage including the symbols involved like the attire, the purpose of religious official and the rings, from an intellectual perspective. It might deter the steadily climbing divorce rate. This means that the effectiveness of the ritual rest in the number of times it is repeated and the understanding of the symbols used in the ritual.

However, if an individual is forced to accept an observable fact that contradicts or conflicts with the ritualized belief, it creates a "loss of faith" feeling. The number one reason most people begin to leave a religion is usually over the subject of sex, which many organized religions have desperately tried to suppress. Even in organizations, when an individual initiated into a group discovers that all of the members do not have the same conviction, they feel a "loss of faith" in the group as well.

Some of the simplest, yet most powerful rituals that can be performed are to regularly venerate your spirits. The following are generalized invocations that will help you to establish a rapport with your spirits. Invocations are different from prayers because certain parts can actually be intoned, repeated and/or chanted.

To perform, simply light a small white birthday candle to the spirit and repeat the prayer in the morning before heading to work. If you can get a candle in the spirit's color this will make your ritual more effective but it is not necessary. Perform the ritual the number times indicated and follow your intuition. Note that once a spiritual connection has begun between you and your spirit. You can talk to your spirits as you would a good friend. You may also get the hunch to purchase and offer certain items for your spirits like cool water, cigars, incense, perfume, etc. Your spirits will not request something that you can't afford or that you will feel uncomfortable purchasing. They certainly will not request that you do something illegal. Use commonsense and keep in mind what was said about synchronicity. Know that if you live your life according to Maa, your spirits will too.

Aakhu
(General Ancestor & Spirit Guide Invocation)

> Oh Almighty Nebertcher, Bless the aakhu with strength, wisdom and light, so that they will continue to be a good and strong support.

Aakhu, I pay homage to you whose shoulders I stand upon. I offer you light for warmth and water to quench your thirst. I ask that you share your wisdom with me, so that we can all overcome the difficulties in our life.

Papa or Uncle Spirits
for Help with Family Issues

> Oh, Great Uncle who has preserved the knowledge and wisdom of our family. Thank you for your sacrifice and support met. Guide me perfectly on this straight path, so that I do not meet with ill fate. Keep me and my loved ones away from all forms of iniquity that would threaten my peace. Help me to remain true, so that my life will continue to honor you. (Offer a white candle. If offering food, remember aakhu don't like salt).

Auntie & Mamma Spirits
for Help with Mothering Issues

> Oh Great Mother, who watches over us all, in these times of uncertainty, help me to survive. Teach me your wise ways and the knowledge of great mother's

past. Give me the strength to resist evil, so that I may hold my hold my head up high. Show me the way to succeed when no way seems possible. Thank you Great Mother. (Offer a white candle. Remember if offering food, the aakhu don't like salt).

Black Hawk

Thank you Black Hawk for sitting high upon the wall and protecting my cultural tradition. (Offer sugar water, white candle and cigar).

Osar for Peace, Knowledge & Wisdom

Now that you know who the real Lord is of your superconscious, you may want to incorporate this nightly ritual to protect yourself and others from negative influences. It is the reciting of the Lord's Prayer. This prayer said in the right mindset should cause you to identify yourself as a Child of Osar.

> Our Father, who art in heaven, hallowed be Thy name, Thy kingdom come, Thy will be done, on earth as it is in heaven. Give us this day, our daily bread, and forgive us trespasses, as we forgive those who trespass against us, and lead us not into temptation, but deliver us from evil. For thou is the kingdom, the power, the glory, forever. Amen[11].

At the end you can make a special request if needed. Note also that any of the biblical scriptures that speak of the "Lord" can be dissected and used as part of an invocation for

---

[11] This last section I learned was usually only repeated by priest, but in the Pentecostal tradition everyone was encouraged to repeat this last segment of the prayer.

Osar. Use a white candle but not necessary since Osar is our primary guardian angel that is with us all the time and everywhere we go.

Npu for General or Devotional Purposes

Divine messenger to us all. Opener of the Way and guardian of the path, open way the door for me, and close those doors and paths that will led to my demise.

Djahuti for Wisdom

Djahuti, show me how to solve this problem.
Thank you.

Oset General Invocation

Sow within me the seeds of fertility, so that everywhere I walk. I reflect Osar's glory. Cover me with your sweet and loving grace. Protect your child so that he (or she) can reclaim the kingdom and restore peace and wisdom to the earth.

Oset protector of children and Divine Mother to us all, bless me with a child The same way you mourned Osar in order to give birth to change. Help me to conceive a child that will bring peace and wisdom into my life.

Nebhet for Happiness

Oh beautiful Nebhet, guardian of love, beauty and wealth. Walk with me as I walk this lonely road in search of our Osar. Cover me in your honey and let all that shimmers before me fall into my hands. Let joy and happiness flow my heart, so that I shine as you do. Thank you. Light a yellow candle.

Nebhet for Love

Nebhet, bring me with the right man (woman) who is in perfect harmony with me. I know it is a spiritual union blessed by you Nebhet because it is divine love functioning through us and bringing us together perfectly. I know I can give this man (woman) the joy, light, love and peace and I believe I can make this man's (woman's) life complete and whole.

Thank you for blessing him (her) to be faithful, loyal, spiritual, true and a happy, harmonious and peaceful man (woman) to be around. We are irresistibly attracted to one another because we are each other's compliment. Anoint our senses with the sweetness of your beauty, love and truth, so that we are attracted to each other right now.

Repeat several times while burning a yellow candle. Repeat ritual for five days. Preferably begin on Friday, Nebhet's day.

Nebhet as St. Martha for Strength

Oh beautiful and strong Nebhet, former wife of Set. Just like you refused to take any more abuse, I call upon you to help me to be victorious over him that brings me misery. Give me good health and steady work so that I can cover my needs. Give me a strong heart and a firm mind so that I can triumph over this

173

beast. Hear me oh great mother. Help me to be triumphant. Amen. (Light a green candle. Can also use St. Martha's image)

Hru for Empowerment

Oh Powerful and true heir of Osar!
Oh Powerful and true heir of Osar!
Hru! Victorious lord and champion for us all.
Gaze upon the evil before me and strike down this enemy! For too long evil has triumphed and kept us all subservient. Oh Powerful and true heir of Osar!
Restore peace, wisdom and happiness to your father's throne! Make us victorious over your enemy!

Hru as St. Barbara for Success

St. Barbara is often identified as being an incarnation of solar spirits like Hru because of her strong will and determination. Papa taught me that Shango the Yoruba incarnation of Hru, is always concerned about winning the war, not the battle. This means that true leaders will sacrifice their pride if need be in order to achieve an objective. This is why the biblical King David and other heroes and heroines all are syncretized with this solar archetype. Like most Hru incarnations, there is always some form of sacrifice that sometimes leads to martyrdom as in the case with St. Barbara.

I have heard several versions of her story so, I will tell you the version that I identified with the most to get the gist of what Hru is about. According to legend in the 4th century Barbara was a beautiful woman that would not marry so King Dioscorus locked her up in the tower. In solitude Barbara is said to have just prayed, studied and eventually she converted to Christianity. Enraged by her conversion,

174

Dioscorus denounced her in front of a formal tribunal where she was later tortured and beheaded by her father Dioscorus. Upon her death, a flash of lightning struck Dioscorus and killed him, while Barbara ascended to the heavens.

Saint (Santa) Barbara can be called upon specifically to bring love, help in conquering obstacles and enemies. Like Hru, she promotes success in all aspects of life and be considered Hru's bride or Hru's sister.

> Santa Barbara bride of Hru.
> The same way you refused to be controlled. Give me the power to resist that which imprisons me. Bring them down to their knees. Give me total victory!

Sokar for Cleansing as San Alejo (St. Alex)

There are two associations I learned of in regards to San Alejo. The first is that in the Curanderismo (Latin American healing traditions) of Mexico and Puerto Rico, the term alejo is closely related to the verb alejar, which means "to make far". Therefore, alejo implies to make someone or something move away from you. The second association is due to his legend, which is said that Alejo was born to rich Roman parents. At an early age he left home and lived his life as beggar, as an act of penance. After 17 years, he returned home but his parents didn't recognize him. So they hired him as a servant, worked him very hard, forced him to sleep under the staircase and they barely fed him. Eventually because of his poor living conditions and miserable circumstances Alejo became deathly ill. On his deathbed, Alejo finally revealed to his parents who he really was and just before passing he forgave them.

I learned in Mexico people often say, "rézale a San Alejo p'a que se te quite lo pendejo" - "pray to San Ajelo so that you might not be so stupid". Whatever the case, San Alejo as an incarnation of Sokar surely helped me to not be an idiot and take my health for granted by entrusting it with anyone.

> Sokar, chase away evil from me. Chase away evil from my doorsteps. Chase away liars, backstabbers and those with forked tongues. Chase away evil thoughts and those with ill intent who envy my heart. Chase evil away and cover with me your protective grace, so that I may honor our lord with me presence. (Offer a white candle. Use a hand broom for sweeping and/or cleansing herbs.)

Sokar as San Lazaro (Saint Lazarus)

There are two Lazarus mentioned in the bible. One is from the parable that Jesus spoke of and the other is from Bethany. Both are often combined together in the minds of many because they were both considered to be poor men. According to the parable, which is said to be a Kamitic folktale about Osar (Elazar or El-Osar-us, later Lazarus), Lazarus is described as a poor man covered with soars that sat a rich man's gate. When the beggar died the angels carried him to heaven and when the rich man died, he was sent to hades where he was tormented. When the rich man asked that Lazarus dip his finger in water to cool his tongue, Abraham reminded the rich man of the way he treated Lazarus. Abraham tells the rich man that a great abyss has been created preventing Lazarus from helping him. So, the rich man cries out that Lazarus warn his brothers to avoid being tormented as he. Abraham denies the rich man's request and tells him that the living have Moses and the

176

prophets. The rich man tells Abraham that if the living sees the dead they will repent.

Lazarus is known for making people change their ways once they see the grave errors that they have made. Often times the Lazarus from the parable is also merged with the Lazarus of Bethany who was resurrected from the dead, because both are associated with rebirth and death. I always tell Sokar the following:

"Thank you for perfect health," while visualizing the things I would do if I was in perfect health. You only need one end result to focus upon.

Hru Aakhuti for General Protection

Hru Aakhuti protect these surroundings. Surround us with your wall of fire and keep within safe from harm. Recite while pouring rum libations on the ground to form an enclosure. (Offer a red candle).

Maat for Increasing Wealth

Nebhet is the guardian over riches, while Maat is considered the guardian over wealth. The difference is that riches can be gained and loss in a flash, wealth is accumulated over a period of time due to calculated decisions. Wealth is a form of financial security, so if you are tired of trying to make ends meet and tired of living paycheck to paycheck. Call upon Maat to help you to grow wealth. If you overspend she will help you to cut back and consider what you need. If you don't spend enough or hoard your money, she will help you to learn how to share. It is suggested that you read Thomas J. Stanley's *The Millionaire Next Door*, T. Harv Eker's *Secrets of the Millionaire Mind* and *The Wealthy Barber* by David Chilton. Say this simple invocation over your money or paycheck.

> Maat, you who can see the cause and effects of all things, bring balance and order into my life. I respect money and I happily spend it constructively, so it returns to me effortlessly a thousand folds. Thank you for helping me to build a financial foundation Maat.

It is important that you do this every time you get paid or before you spend your money. The problem most people have when it comes for asking for money is that they do it when they don't have any money in their pockets. Likes attract likes, so when you have money in your pockets, this is the best time to attract more money. For added potency (not necessary) anoint your cash money and billfold with honeysuckle oil.

Thwarting Set

I hope you see by now that there are three aspects of yourself. Your Set symbolizing everything that you have learned including your ego is necessary in order for you to survive, but at the same time. Your Set can be your greatest opposition. One of Set's major powers is the power of guilt, which he uses only a regular basis to control us all, because he is the lord of mischief, chaos and confusion.

Take for instance the subject of tithing, which was a practice initiated years ago by the first hunters and gatherers. The psychology of it is that you offer ten percent to avoid spoiling the whole 100%. In our contemporary times, our Set will make us feel bad if we do not share what we have earned with others especially the less fortunate. This guilt feeling alone is enough to sabotage our best conscious efforts to advance in any way. So, the remedy is to tithe. By tithing 10% of your earnings to a nonprofit organization, when Set uses guilt to make it appear that you haven't shared anything. You can fight him with reasoning by indicating that you paid your spiritual insurance.

Tithing is one of the old spiritual tools that many of us need to employ because a lot of us have been scarred into believing that wealth is filthy, evil, etc. If we were to tithe with the idea in mind that we will be protected, it would counter Set's actions. Tithing works because it is based upon Maa, which focuses upon being proactive. I like to think of tithing in another way because since there are nine netcharu (not counting Set who makes up the tenth). I like to think of the ten percent as being Set and the other 90% being the netcharu, so by tithing I am thrilled to do something that will counteract Set's chaos, confusion and mischief. This is the reason for offering 10% to any nonprofit organization because you should be excited and just thrilled to be in the position to give money to another to help others.

This is one of the reasons libations and food offerings are practiced throughout Africa and Asia, because it is believed only hungry spirits (aapepu) cause accidents. So alcohol is offered to the spirits, to encourage them not to cause any chaos, confusion and mischief. When people are not able to make a formal offering a prayer is offered instead, a tradition that continues to this day amongst many African American churches in the southern part of the United States.

So thwart Set's influence by saying a prayer, making an offering or tithing to prevent chaos, confusion and mischief. Remember, Set is not the epitome of evil. He is just raw, uncontrollable, chaotic and confused energy that can appear anytime and anywhere. Doing something to counteract his energy is a great way of muster spiritual power.

The reason I wanted to include this is because some of us are sitting on top of billion dollars dreams and ideas, but will not take the first step because we're afraid. The purpose of writing this is to help push you in the right direction so that you can accomplish your dreams. Set exists to force you to be real with yourself. He plays the antagonist in our life, so that we can become the protagonist. It is the only way we can become great. So keep this in mind every time you are faced with a difficult decision or some form of opposition that it exist to challenge you to be a divine child.

In Conclusion

As always I try to end every book with something positive and uplifting pertaining to the Maa Aankh, so keeping with tradition. When I first wrote Maa Aankh volume one, at the end of the journey, I found myself at the Jamestown museum in Virginia face to face with an African carved rosary that martyrized Queen Nzingah as a saint. It was a real connection and proof that I was being led by my ancestors. This is how I learned that too much emphasis is placed on our physical being, but we can't ignore it. Again, it is natural to be skeptic, which is why I like many African descendants was always curious about my ethnicity. So, one day while surfing the web I came across a small interview on one of my favorite singers Erykah Badu. Now, I had been following Erykah since the beginning because a lot of times entertainers reflect and verify the energy and consciousness that is present in the world. For instance, Erykah's debut album consisted of a lot of Supreme Mathematics based upon the teachings of the Five Percent Nation. During this time, there were a lot of people whose lives were improved and they could relate to what she was saying on a mundane and deeper intellectual level. This is why I continued to support her music and the last time I saw an interview on her, she had gone to Cuba. This around the same time I had finished writing *Maa Aankh* volumes I and II. As I listened to the interview she spoke of her experience with the Santeros (priests and priestesses in Santeria), which was verification of my experience with Papa.

The latest interview I saw of Ms. Erykah was of her receiving her DNA results back. I took the interview as confirmation from the Spirit(s) that I needed to do the test and put some closure on some things. So, I submitted a swab of my DNA and I just received my results the day after I finished writing this book. Come to find out, my ethnic background is 84% African – 28% Ivory Coast/Ghana, 26% Cameroon/Congo, 10% Benin/Togo, 10% Senegalese and 9% Southeastern Bantu with the remaining percentage coming from Europe and Asia. Like most people upon receiving this news, I was shocked because the Native American marker was not present. I learned later that the test simply shows what DNA traits were passed down to me. It didn't mean that one of my ancestors was not Native American, so this was a relief especially to my parents who are trying to retrieve records on my great grandmother.

However, I was amazed because it validated everything that I had said about the Africans not being able to practice their indigenous spiritual beliefs, so they relied upon those from the Kongo – Angolan region (present day Cameroon and Congo). It revealed that I didn't just dream or conjure the Maa Aankh. It was verification and proof that it was my ancestors that passed this cosmogram down to me. And, why did they pass it down to me? Because, I believe my ancestors saw the conditions of our current state of affairs. They saw how devastated the Congo and other parts of Africa are right now. I seriously believe that my ancestors understood that I wanted to help my loved ones and in order for me to do that. I had to go beyond my Cuban brothers and sisters' interpretation of the Kongo system and recognize my ancestors' in the United States perspective. Along with observing a more unadulterated form that existed in Kamit. Basically, I believe my ancestors helped me because saw that I wanted to be saved and I accepted the fact that I am the only one who could save me, so they blessed me with the Maa Aankh cosmology.

I didn't need a test but I am glad that the test confirmed that I truly am an Afrikan in America. I know now that slavery didn't make my history but it interrupted me from making history. Thankfully, through this spiritual work, I have reclaimed mine's back.

It is my hope that this book serve as a guide in helping you to reclaim your power and whatever was lost. I wish you all well in your journey, until next time. Peace.

Selected Bibliography

Amen, Ra Un Nefer. *Metu Neter Vol. 1: The Great Oracle of Tehuti and the Egyptian System of Spiritual Cultivation.* Khamit Media Trans Visions Inc, 1990

Browder, Anthony T. *From the Browder File: 22 Essays on the African American Experience.* Institute of Karmic Guidance, 1989.

Browder, Anthony T. *Nile Valley Contributions to Civilization.* Institute of Karmic Guidance, 1992.

Budge, E.A. Wallis. *An Egyptian Hieroglyphic Dictionary Vol. I and II.* New York: Dover Publication, 1978.

Budge, E.A. Wallis. *Osiris & The Egyptian Resurrection, vols. 1 & 2.* Dover Publications, 1973.

Chadwick, David and Suzuki, Shunryu *To Shine One Corner of the World: Moments with Shunryu Suzuki.* Broadway; 2001.

Eker, T. Harv. Secrets of the Millionaire Mind: Mastering the Inner Game of Wealth. *HarperBusiness, 2005.*

Fu-Kiau, K. Kia Bunseki. *African Cosmology of the Bantu-Kongo: Principles of Life & Living.* Athelia Henrietta Press, 2001.

Harner, Michael. *The Way of the Shaman.* Harper One; 10 Anv. edition, 1980

Hollenweger, W. J. *The Pentecostals: The Charismatic Movement in the Churches.* Augsburg Publishing House, 1972.

Kurzweil, R. 2012. How To Create A Mind: The Secret of Human Thought Revealed. New York: Penguin Group.

MacGaffey, Wyatt. *Custom and Government in the Lower Congo.* University of California Press, 1970.

MacGaffey, Wyatt. *Religion and Society in Central Africa: The BaKongo of Lower Zaire.* The University of Chicago Press, 1986.

Melody, and Julianne Guilbault. *Love is in the Earth: A Kaleidoscope of Crystals - The Reference Book Describing the Metaphysical Properties of the Mineral Kingdom.* Earth Love Pub House; Updated, 3rd edition (1995).

Moore, Derric. *Kamta: A Practical Kamitic Path for Obtaining Power.* Four Sons Publications, 2011

Moore, Derric. *Maa: A Guide to the Kamitic Way for Personal Transformation.* Four Sons Publications, 2012

Moore, Derric. *Maa Aankh: MAA AANKH: Finding God the Afro-American Spiritual Way, by Honoring the Ancestors and Guardian Spirits.* Four Sons Publications, 2010

Moore, Derric. *Maa Aankh: MAA AANKH:* Discovering the Power of I AM Using the Shamanic Principles of Ancient Egypt for Self-Empowerment and Personal Development. Four Sons Publication, 2013

Synan, Vinson. *The Holiness-Pentecostal Movement in the United States.* William B. Eerdmans Publishing Company, 1971.

Thompson, Robert Farris. *Flash of the Spirit: African and Afro-American Art and Philosophy.* Random House, 1983.

Thompson, Robert Farris. *Face of the Gods: Art and Altars of Africa and the African Americas.* Prestel, 1993.

Thornton, John. *Africa and Africans in the Making of the Atlantic World, 1400-1800.* Cambridge University Press; 2 ed., 1998.

Index

Author's Note

Thank you for allowing me to share my experience, story, and methods that I have found that worked for me with you. I hope that it empowered and improved your life the way it has touched mine.

If you enjoyed the book and have a minute to spare, I would really appreciate an honest review on the page or site where you purchase the book. Your review is greatly appreciated because reviews from readers like you, make a huge difference in helping new readers find practical spiritual books like this one.

Amazon Review: https://amzn.to/2XUhOP9

1 SoL Alliance.com: http://bit.ly/32uJ9e4

Thank you!

Derric "Rau Khu" Moore

Other Books by the Author:

MAA AANKH Volume I:
Finding God the Afro-American Spiritual Way,
by Honoring the Ancestors and Guardian Spirits

Kamta: A Practical Kamitic Path for Obtaining Power

Maa: A Guide to the Kamitic Way for Personal Transformation

MAA AANKH Volume II:
Discovering the Power of I AM Using the Shamanic Principles of
Ancient Egypt for Self-Empowerment and Personal Development

MAA AANKH Volume III:
The Kamitic Shaman Way of Working the Superconscious Mind to
Improve Memory, Solve Problems Intuitively and Spiritually Grow
Through the Power of the Spirits (Volume 3)

Honoring the Ancestors the Kemetic Shaman Way:
A Practical Manual for Venerating and Working with the Ancestors
from a God Perspective

The Kamta Primer: A Practical Shamanic Guide for Using Kemetic
Ritual, Magick and Spirituality for Acquiring Power

En Español: Maa Aankh Volume I:

Encontrando a Dios al Modo Espiritual Afroamericano, Honrando a los

Ancestros y a los Espiritus Guardianes

Neter (God) Got Your Back!

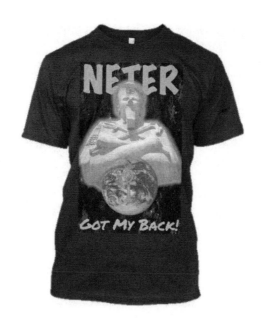

Purchase your empowering, enlightening and uplifting MKBN tees, hoodies and caps today at 1SoLAlliance.com

For more books on religion, astrology, numerology, chakras, prayer, reiki, self-help and metaphysical supplies, visit us at:

www.thelandofkam.com

www.1solalliance.com